STANDING BEAR'S QUEST FOR FREEDOM

First Civil Rights Victory for Native Americans

by

Lawrence A. Dwyer

STANDING BEAR'S QUEST FOR FREEDOM
First Civil Rights Victory for Native Americans

KLD Books, Inc.
Omaha, Nebraska
www.KLDbooks.org

Second Printing, 2020

ISBN: 978-0-9992061-9-5 (book)
ISBN: 978-1-7334218-0-5 (e-book)

Library of Congress Control Number: 2019950299

Cover Photo
Chief Standing Bear, studio portrait, at time of Ponca Chiefs visit with President Hayes, Washington D.C. 1877. Courtesy of History Nebraska RG1227-02-02.

Cover Design
Jillian McClenahan, Anastasia Co.

Note
The word "Indian" is used throughout the book only if from a direct source quote. Otherwise, the words "Native American" are used.

Dedication

Betty Davis
1934 -2018

On a cold day in February 2009, Betty Davis called and invited me to give the keynote address at the 130th Anniversary celebration of the Trial of Standing Bear sponsored by the Douglas County Historical Society. At the time, Betty was Executive Director of the Historical Society and I was a member of the Board of Directors. The Historical Society is headquartered in the Crook House on the grounds of old Fort Omaha where Standing Bear and his fellow Ponca prisoners were held captive in 1879. My research for that talk fired a passion within me to write the story of the Trial of Standing Bear from a lawyer's perspective.

The impetus to write this book began ten years ago at that commemorative event. It would not have happened without Betty's invitation and the insights and encouragement she generously gave to me, even within a month of her death. For that reason, I dedicate this book to my dear friend Betty Davis.

Before We Came – They Were Here
Lawrence A. Dwyer

Before we came - they were here.

Before the Declaration of Independence was signed and
the Constitution enacted –
they were here.

Before Lewis & Clark came –
they were here.

Before our ancestors came to live here –
the ancestors of Standing Bear were here.

Before we came the Poncas –
hunted deer and buffalo,
fished for carp and trout,
planted and harvested corn, beans, and squash,
built their own homes
married and lived in family units,
educated their children,
defended their land,
supported themselves,
healed their sick,
honored their elders,
buried their dead,
remembered past glories,
and dreamed dreams.

Before we came the Poncas were -
living their own way of life – in a manner of their own
choosing,
under their own rules for self-governance,
under their own system of law.

And then we came –
bringing a new system of law.

And the two systems of law collided.

Table of Contents

Prologue

He was not a free man. His people were sick and dying. It had been 18 months since the U.S. government forcibly moved the Ponca Tribe from their homeland near the Niobrara River 500 miles to Indian Territory.[1] He described the painful and unjust environment where the government had placed his people:

> Starvation so reduced our strength that when the sickness came on in the fall they could not stand it, and our people began to die. It was like a great house with a big fire in it, and everything was poison. We never saw such kind of sickness before. One hundred and fifty of our people have died, and more are dying every day. It is the worst country in the world. It was a place made to die in and not to live in. The ground is all hills and the prairie covered with stones. There is no land there which will raise anything, and we have nothing to farm with, for they never brought us the things they took away. We had nothing to do but sit still, be sick, starve and die.[2]

Bear Shield, his teenage son, died. In his final words, he asked his father to take him home to be buried alongside the bones of his ancestors. The Poncas believed that if they were not buried with the bones of their ancestors, they would wander the next world alone. Family and tradition meant everything to the Poncas. Standing Bear, a loving father, promised his son he would take him home.

On January 2, 1879, a few days after Bear Shield's death, hungry, sick, and facing death themselves, Standing Bear and 29 men, women and children left the government-designated Indian Territory (present-day Oklahoma) to return home. His quest for freedom had begun. All Standing Bear had wanted was the right to live and die with his family on his own land – on the beloved land of his Ponca ancestors.

Sixty-two days into their "Journey of Sorrows," Standing Bear and his companions arrived near Decatur, Nebraska, at the village of their cousins, the Omaha tribe. Iron Eye, chief of the Omaha tribe, and his daughter Bright Eyes, greeted them with food, clothing and medical care after seeing their awful condition – frostbite, bleeding feet, gauntness, torn clothing, crying children. Everyone was sick and exhausted. Standing Bear shared with his cousins, the sufferings the Poncas had endured.

Three weeks later, General George Crook, Commander of the Department of the Platte, received an order from his superiors to arrest these Poncas for leaving their reservation without government permission. The soldiers came to the Omaha tribe reservation and escorted the Ponca prisoners to Fort Omaha.

Iron Eye and Bright Eyes made the 100-hundred-mile trip from their Omaha tribe reservation to Fort Omaha, also willing to risk arrest for leaving without government permission. They had to tell General Crook the heartbreaking plight of their cousins.

General Crook was so disturbed by their story that he decided to do something unusual for the arresting officer. Shortly after midnight on March 30, 1879, Crook took Iron Eye and Bright Eyes to see his friend, Thomas Tibbles, deputy editor of the *Omaha Herald* newspaper. They arrived at Tibble's office in downtown Omaha at 1:00 o'clock in the morning. Tibbles reported that General Crook told him, "Now I'm ordered to do a more cruel thing than ever before. I've come to ask if you will not take up the matter." [3]

Tibbles agreed to help. He immediately secured the expertise of attorneys John L. Webster and Andrew J. Poppleton. Together, they devised a strategy to challenge the government's right to hold the Ponca prisoners against their will.

Two months later, Federal District Court Judge Elmer S. Dundy issued a ruling that was unprecedented in American History. The first civil rights victory for Native Americans had been achieved. It all began because of one man – Standing Bear.

Chapter 1

His Name Was Standing Bear

Among his people he was known as *Ma-chu-nah-zha*, sometimes written as Ma-chu-na-zhi.

Photographs taken near the time of the trial confirm the description that John G. Bourke, aide-de-camp to General George Crook, wrote: 'Standing Bear, the head man, was a noble looking Indian, tall and commanding in presence, dignified in manner; very elegantly dressed in the costume of his tribe." [4]

Standing Bear was an eloquent speaker. He could convey his inner feelings in poetic imagery and metaphors, leaving those who heard him mesmerized. To read his speeches, even today, nearly a century and a half later, is to feel his beautiful spirit and kind heart.

Growing up on the land of his ancestors near the Niobrara River within the Nebraska/South Dakota border, Standing Bear listened to his grandparents relate stories of the history and traditions of the Poncas. These stories enhanced the pride he carried for the bravery and determination his ancestors demonstrated as they defended their land, supported their families, and lived their way of life.

All Standing Bear ever wanted was to live and die on his own land.[5] He wanted to pass on these same stories to his grandchildren. It is how it had been done for generations, the Ponca way.

This is a story of a great and noble man:

- ◊ A man who had been robbed of everything by the government, except his pride.
- ◊ A man whose heart was filled with love for his people and the land he called home.
- ◊ A man of courage willing to travel 500 miles in the cold and ice of winter to bury his son in ancestral burial grounds.
- ◊ A man determined to fight for his freedom as a human being.

His name was Standing Bear.

Standing Bear
Courtesy of History Nebraska RG2066.5-2

Chapter 1 - His Name Was Standing Bear

Chapter 2

Early History of the Poncas

To trace the early history of the Poncas is to put together a puzzle. There is a "lack of archeological evidence in the form of a neat string of sites stretching back in time and space to the ancestral homeland of the Poncas; so we must rely upon other sorts of data in reconstructing the tribe's past," as pointed out by ethnologist James H. Howard. [6]

Published reports of the origin and customs of the Ponca tribe by ethnologist James O. Dorsey suggest they were related to the Omaha, Osage, Kaw and Quapaw tribes, living somewhere "east of the Mississippi River."[7] Ethnologists Alice C. Fletcher and Francis LaFlesche lived with the Ponca and Omaha Tribes and suggested their origins may have extended as far East as Virginia and North Carolina.[8]

Alice C. Fletcher, Hartley Burr Alexander,[9] Douglas Scott, Henry P. Eames, Francis LaFlesche, June 5, 1919
Courtesy of History Nebraska RG2026-73

Early writings give different spelling of their name: Poncar, Puncahs, Pana, and Ponkas.[10] Eventually, these five tribes settled in the Ohio River Valley. In the early part of the 16th Century, "some went down the Mississippi, hence arose their name "Quapaw" meaning "down-stream people," the rest ascended the river taking the name "U-ma-ha" (Omaha) meaning "up-stream people." [11]

Ancestral Land

After this separation in the 16th Century, the Ponca and Omaha peoples followed the Missouri River upstream to Pipestone, Minnesota.[12] Because of the scarcity of buffalo and frequent attacks by the Dakota/Sioux, they separated. The Omahas moved into Northeastern Nebraska, and the Poncas settled in the Niobrara River valley on the border of present-day Nebraska and South Dakota.[13] Dorsey believed this final separation "must have occurred before 1673."[14] A published map by cartographer Guillaume de I'Isle in 1718 confirms this location.[15]

The Poncas were a semi-sedentary horticultural people who treasured their ancestral land. The annual buffalo hunt provided them, as well as other Native American tribes, with nearly eighty different uses necessary for their survival:

> Almost everything the Plains Indians owned, wore and used was made in part from the buffalo. Clothing, blankets, moccasin soles, tipi covers, ropes, containers, bags, saddles and glue were all made from buffalo hides, bones or hooves. Buffalo robes were the single irreplaceable source of most of the belongings of all Plains Indian peoples.[16] [17]

The Poncas were such a family-oriented people that the hunters would make certain upon their return home to take care of those members of the tribe who were elderly or otherwise unable to go on the hunt - "they get the most tenderest meat." [18]

They supplemented the annual buffalo hunt with corn, squash, potatoes, native plants, and fish caught in the Niobrara River.[19] Soon they built earth-lodges to provide a sense of permanence for their families. However, the close proximity of their homes within the village left them vulnerable to attacks by neighboring tribes, who could easily surround them. In addition, diseases brought by traders and other visitors could spread rapidly through their village. [20]

Notable Visitors

Over the years, explorers, missionaries, traders (Spanish and French), mercantilists, and painters came to the Ponca villages. A few notable visitors left written memories of their time with them.

Lewis & Clark (1804). In the early months of Lewis & Clark's two-year "Voyage of Discovery," William Clark visited the Ponca village on September 5, 1804, and made the following entry in his journal:

> Set out early, the winds blew hard from the south as it has for some days past, we set up a jury mast & sailed, I saw a large gangue of turkeys, also grous seen ... saw several wild goats on the cliff and deer with black tales. Sent Shields & Gibson to the Poncas Towns, which is situated on the Ponca River on the lower side about two miles from its mouth in an open butifull Plain, at this time this Nation is out hunting biffalow.[21]

Although Lewis & Clark never had a chance to sit down with the Ponca people, they estimated a population of about 200 members, having been "reduced by smallpox and their war with the Soues."[22]

Lewis & Clark separated after their historic journey. Meriwether Lewis died just a few years later in 1809. William Clark went on to a distinguished career in public service, including negotiating the first treaty between the United States and the Ponca Tribe in 1817. Later he was appointed Superintendent of Indian Affairs by President Monroe with headquarters in St. Louis, Missouri. There, he met George Catlin.

George Catlin (1832). After practicing law for a few years in his native Pennsylvania, Catlin went West with a strong desire to study the life and customs of the various Plains Indian Tribes and paint their portraits. Arriving in St. Louis in 1830, he met Clark who took him on visits to tribes living near the Missouri River. Two years later, Catlin boarded the American Fur Company's steamboat Yellowstone for a voyage up the Missouri River. He disembarked at the Ponca village to live with them for a few months.[23]

The Ponca tribe was very small when Catlin arrived, so it is likely he met most of the people, possibly including three-year-old Standing Bear.

In his journal, which accompanied his paintings, Catlin provides us with an eyewitness account of the life and customs of Standing Bear's people noting they numbered less than 500 living in 80 earth lodges. He painted portraits of more than 300 members of the various tribes he visited. He was especially drawn to Shoo-de-ga-cha (Smoke), Chief of the Ponca tribe whom he painted wearing his full buffalo-robe, saying:

> He is a noble specimen of native dignity and philosophy. I conversed much with him, and from his dignified manners, as well as from the soundness of his reasoning, I became fully convinced that he deserved to be the sachem of a more numerous and prosperous tribe. [24]

Prince Maximillian & Karl Bodner (1833). Within a year of Catlin's visit, the renowned German explorer, ethnologist and naturalist Maximillian, Prince Von Wied (1782-1867) visited the Ponca tribe, accompanied by watercolor painter, Karl Bodner of Switzerland. With the assistance of William Clark, they journeyed up the Missouri River and stayed in the Ponca village for a few weeks in May 1833. [25]

Note: Prince Maximillian's Diary of his journey, and many of Bodner's paintings of Native Americans are displayed in Omaha's Joslyn Art Museum.

Summary

The written records of these visitors describe a group of semi-sedentary horticultural people led by noble chiefs. The Poncas were the smallest tribe in the region. The government's 1780 census listed their population at 800.[26] In 1804 Lewis & Clark estimated their population at around 200.[27]

Somehow, despite epidemic diseases and attacks by neighboring tribes, the Poncas survived, a peaceful and honorable people, proud and determined to live and die on their own land.

Chapter 2 - Early History of the Poncas

Chapter 3

The Ponca System of Law

The Ponca Tribe developed a system of law based on their own customs and rules of conduct, evident by the way they governed themselves. The meaning of "law" was defined in *State v. Central Lumber Co,* 123 NW 504 (SD 1909):

> The great and only excusable reason for the prescribing of any rule of conduct is to promote justice between man and his fellows in their relations as members of a social or political body. Law may be defined as the aggregate of those rules and principles of conduct promulgated by the legislative authority or established by local custom, and our laws are the resultant derived from a combination of the divine or moral laws, the laws of nature, and human experience....The effort to promote and effectuate justice by means of human laws has been a continuous fight against human selfishness, especially human avarice and greed, a continual effort to protect the weak against the strong. [28]

According to this definition, the Ponca tribe was a law-abiding society that promoted order, rules of conduct, and justice amongst its people.

Rules of Conduct

Tribal historian and interpreter, Peter LeClaire was of Ponca descent and he shared his own study, *Ponca History,* with ethnologist James Howard in 1949. Howard said that "this interesting document contains, in addition to the oral historical traditions of the tribe, a great deal of material on the customs, morals, and attitudes of the Ponca of his own and earlier generations."[29]

LeClaire summarized for Howard the seven basic principles that guided the Poncas' rules of conduct for the governance of their society:

1) Have one god
2) Do not kill one another
3) Do not steal from one another
4) Be kind to one another
5) Do not talk about each other
6) Do not be stingy
7) Have respect for the Sacred Pipe[30]

Organization

The Ponca tribe was organized into kinship groups known as clans (bands) built along paternal bloodlines. Each clan was led by its own chief and had certain assigned duties for the overall benefit of the tribe.[31] At the time of the Standing Bear trial, there were nine clans.[32] Standing Bear was chief of the Bear Clan. White Eagle was the Paramount Chief of the tribe. Photographs of Standing Bear often show him wearing a necklace of bear claws to signify his role in this clan and his position of tribal leadership.

The Ponca system of law was based on the simple philosophy that what was good for the tribe as a whole was of benefit for each member. The central governing body of chiefs encouraged a division of labor, a common system of beliefs, individual accountability, and a desire to preserve and pass on their customs and traditions. Ethnologist Alice C. Fletcher reported that the chiefs were responsible for "maintaining peace and order within the tribe and making peace with other tribes." [33]

The chiefs made decisions which they "enforced by a group called the Buffalo-Police (because their greatest period of activity came during the tribal hunts). The chiefs attempted to act at all times in accordance with public opinion. Complete, or nearly complete, unanimity was necessary before any action would be taken. [34]

The Sacred Pipe

The Sacred Pipe was an important instrument in Ponca society. When a member of the tribe broke a rule of conduct, the chiefs often assembled in a circle around the paramount chief as a sign of unity. They smoked the Sacred Pipe to allow the emotions of opposing parties to calm, before they arrived at a decision imposing an appropriate penalty.[35] For example:

◊ Punishment for thievery was either restitution,[36] or whipping.[37]

◊ Punishment for adultery was often left to the injured spouse to decide.[38]

◊ Punishment for deliberate murder was usually banishment from the tribe for a number of years, unless the man was sooner forgiven by the relatives of the murdered man.[39]

◊ Punishment for disturbing the buffalo herd prior to the tribe's coordinated attack was whipping. Sometimes after the hunt was over and the offender had returned to the village with the rest of the tribe, the Buffalo-Police would "give him gifts so that his heart would not be bad." In this way, the offender was "reincorporated into society." [40]

The correlation between breaking a rule of conduct and the penalty imposed reflected the Poncas respect for each other and their desire to promote the common good of the tribe, seeking "conformity, not revenge."[41]

Summary

The historical evidence supports the belief that prior to their forced removal in 1877 to Indian Territory, the Poncas lived and worked under their own system of law based on: 1) known rules of conduct for behavior; 2) organized clans with designated leaders and duties; 3) a council of chiefs who governed and employed the Buffalo Police to enforce their decisions; 4) a semi-sedentary life dwelling in permanent housing; 5) horticultural plantings for food, supplemented with periodic buffalo hunts; and 6) family life that nurtured their children and respected their elders

The Poncas were a law-abiding, civilized people desiring to be left alone to work their land in peace and to be buried among their beloved ancestors.

The government did not bring law and civilization to the Poncas, it brought its power and, eventually, the military.

Chapter 4

The American System of Law - Supreme Court Cases & Legislation

As the government imposed its power and will upon the Poncas, the two legal systems collided.

◊ The Ponca system of law was simple and efficient.

◊ In stark contrast, the American system of law was a mixture of court rulings, congressional legislation and treaties.

Supreme Court Cases

Two rulings of the United States Supreme Court in early years of the 19th Century had disastrous repercussions for Native Americans.

Doctrine of Discovery. In 1823, the case of *Johnson and Graham's Lessee v. William M'Intosh* 21 U.S. 543 (1823) came before the United States Supreme Court. The facts of the case are that private citizen Thomas Johnson "purchased" land in 1775 from a Native American Tribe, the Piankeshaws. His descendants filed an action in the District Court of Illinois to eject William M'Intosh from "their" land. M'Intosh refused to leave alleging that he was the rightful owner holding a land patent from the federal government granted to him in 1818. Thus, two parties claimed ownership to the same tract of land, each claiming they had received title and ownership rights from different grantors: one grantor being a Native American Tribe, and the other grantor being the United States Government.

John Marshall, Chief Justice of the United States Supreme Court, affirmed the decision of the lower court in favor of M'Intosh. In his decision, Justice Marshall adopted the European "doctrine of discovery" in relation to Native American tribes, saying:

> They remain in a state of nature, and have never been admitted into the general society of nations ... Discovery is the foundation of title, in European nations, and this overlooks all proprietary rights in the natives ... Even if it should be admitted that the Indians were originally an independent people, they have ceased to be so. A nation that has passed under the dominion of another, is no longer a sovereign state ... The subjection proceeds from their residence within our territory and jurisdiction. It is unnecessary to show that they are not citizens in the ordinary sense of that term since they are destitute of the most essential rights which belong to that character. They are of that class who are said by jurists not to be citizens, but perpetual inhabitants with diminutive rights. The Statutes of Virginia and of all the other colonies, and of the United States, treat them as an inferior race of people, without the privileges of citizens and under the perpetual protection and pupilage of the government. [42]

Justice Marshall further wrote that our new American Republic assumed the same right the European nations had claimed when the colonies defeated the British at Yorktown in 1781:

> By the treaty which concluded the war of our revolution, Great Britain relinquished all claim, not only to the government, but to the 'propriety and territorial rights of the United States,' whose boundaries were fixed in the second article. By this treaty, the powers of government, and the right to soil, which had previously been in Great Britain, passed definitively to these States....It has never been doubted, that either the United States, or the several States, had a clear title to all the lands within the boundary

> lines described in the treaty, subject only to the Indian right of occupancy, and that the exclusive power to extinguish that right was vested in that government which might constitutionally exercise it. [43]

Wards of the Government. The second major United States Supreme Court decision affecting the Poncas and other tribes was the case of *The Cherokee Nation v. The State of Georgia* 30 U.S.1 (GA. 1831), in which Justice John Marshall held:

> They may, more correctly perhaps, be denominated domestic dependent nations. They occupy a territory to which we assert a title independent of their will, which must take effect in point of possession when their right of possession ceases. Meanwhile they are in a state of pupilage. Their relation to the United States resembles that of a ward to his guardian. [44]

So, in Justice Marshall's thinking, the powerful words of equality and freedom found in the Declaration of Independence likely did not include the original inhabitants of this land:

> We hold these truths to be self-evident, that all men are created equal, that they are endowed by their creator with certain unalienable rights, that among these are life, liberty and the pursuit of happiness. That to secure these rights, governments are instituted among men, deriving their just powers from the consent of the governed. [45]

Congressional Legislation

In addition to these two Supreme Court rulings, Congress enacted legislation in the 19th Century that had adverse consequences for Native Americans, especially those tribes living west of the Mississippi River.

Bureau of Indian Affairs. In 1824, the Bureau of Indian Affairs was created under the jurisdiction of the War Department for the purpose of making treaties with various tribes. The Bureau's operations were transferred to the newly created Department of the Interior in 1849.[46] The intrusion into the life of the Poncas and other tribes by Agents and Inspectors of the Bureau was marked by unkept promises, and long delays in delivering annuities and goods promised to them by the government. [47]

Indian Removal Act. In 1830, Congress granted the President authority to negotiate treaties with Indian tribes living west of the Mississippi River, for their removal to "Indian Territory," present-day Oklahoma.[48]

Kansas-Nebraska Act. In 1854, Congress enacted the Kansas-Nebraska Act which would change the landscape of American politics forever, eventually leading to a Civil War. The issue of possible expansion of slavery into the Great Plains forced both the North and the South to encourage people to move into the area, since the issue would be decided by local vote, the so-called idea of "popular sovereignty". The issues presented by this Act brought Abraham Lincoln into the forefront of the national discussion, propelling him into the White House seven years later. [49]

Homestead Act. In 1862, Congress promised to grant a free tract of land to anyone over 21 who had not taken up arms against the government, provided they made improvements to the land and stayed on it for five years. [50]

Summary

As a result of these legislative acts, a massive influx of pro-slavery and anti-slavery activists, as well as homesteaders in search of a new life, came into the Nebraska Territory prior to and following the Civil War. They all had different motives for coming, but the result was the same: they encroached on tribal lands and disturbed the buffalo's natural habitat.

To promote and accommodate these new settlers, the government likely felt justified in moving some of the tribes onto smaller reservations and eventually to Indian Territory. One of the major reasons this happened was because Justice Marshall had embedded into the American Legal System these two principles:

1) Native Americans were "to be treated as an inferior race of people...under the perpetual protection and pupilage of the government," like "that of a ward to his guardian."

2) "Discovery is the foundation of title," therefore Native Americans had "the right to possess the land they occupy," but "the exclusive power to extinguish that right was vested in the government...independent of their will."

Therefore, the American legal system considered Native Americans "wards," not persons; and "occupants" of the land they lived on, not its owners. The Poncas and other Native American tribes could be moved at any time, to anyplace, at the will of the government.

They were like pieces on a chessboard.

Chapter 4 – The American System of Law - Cases

Chapter 5

The American System of Law - Treaties

In addition to Supreme Court rulings and Congressional legislation, the American System of Law included treaties made with Native American tribes. The guiding principle in dealing with these tribes after America won its independence was set out in the Northwest Ordinance.

The Northwest Ordinance - 1787

On July 13, 1787, two years before the US Constitution was effective and in force, the Continental Congress enacted the Northwest Ordinance for dealing with Native American tribes. The Ordinance said.

> The utmost **good faith** shall always be observed towards the Indians; their lands and property shall never be taken from them without their consent; and, in their property, rights, and liberty, they never shall be invaded or disturbed, unless in just and lawful wars authorized by Congress; but laws founded in justice and humanity, shall from time to time be made for preventing wrongs being done to them, and for preserving peace and friendship with them. [51]

In English Common Law, good faith "applies to the negotiation, the agreement itself, and the manner in which the treaty is performed. It involves both action and intention. It is based entirely upon honesty, which is required of all parties to a treaty." [52]

The Northwest Ordinance used absolute language such as, "shall always" and "shall never," to declare its intent to respect Native Americans as owners of their land. Justice Marshall's justification for the "doctrine of discovery" ignored the intent and spirit of the Northwest Ordinance. If the government in the 19th century had believed in these same ideals, the lives of the Poncas and other tribes would likely have been very different.

The United States Constitution - 1789

The United States Constitution continued the principle of good faith set out in the Northwest Ordinance and established the paramount authority of an executed treaty:

> *Article VI.* This constitution, and the laws of the United States which shall be made in pursuance thereof; and all treaties made, or which shall be made, the authority of the United States, shall be the supreme law of the land; and the judges in every state shall be bound thereby, anything in the Constitution or laws of any State to the contrary notwithstanding. [53]

The Constitution also provided a protocol for the three branches of government to follow in the treaty-making process, with its built-in delays that would later prove difficult for the Poncas:

> Executive Branch. Article II. Section 2. gave sole authority for treaty-making to the executive branch of the Government stating that "the President shall have power, by and with the advice and consent of the Senate, to make treaties, provided two-thirds of the Senators present concur."[54]

> Congressional Branch. Article I. Section 8. stated that "the Congress shall have the power...to regulate commerce with foreign nations, and among the several states, and with the Indian Tribes."[55]

> Judicial Branch. Article III. Section 2. stated that "the judicial power shall extend to all cases, in law and equity, arising under this Constitution, the laws of the United States, and treaties made."[56]

In 1801, the Supreme Court affirmed the authority of the constitution in this matter holding in *United States v. Schooner Peggy* that "the constitution of the United States declares a treaty to be the supreme law of the land; of consequence its obligation on the courts of the United States must be admitted."[57]

Treaties with The Poncas

The United States negotiated 374 treaties with Native American tribes after the Constitution went into effect in 1789. Four of these treaties were entered into with the Ponca tribe: 1817, 1825, 1858 and 1865. The Poncas never broke a treaty - the government did.

The Ponca Treaty of 1817. The Poncas signed their first treaty with the government on June 25, 1817. Chief Shu-de-ga-xe (Smoke), the same chief George Catlin painted and wrote about in 1832, was one of the signers. The government, represented by William Clark and Auguste Chouteau, initiated this first treaty because it wanted to establish a mutual relationship with the Poncas based upon "perpetual peace and friendship." [58]

The Ponca Treaty of 1825. The second treaty was signed by the Poncas on June 9, 1825. Chief Shu-de-ga-xe (Smoke), was again one of the signers. General Henry Atkinson and Major Benjamin O'Fallon signed on behalf of the government. The Atkinson-O'Fallon Journal entry reported that as the parties came together in an open field, General Atkinson led his troops and band in a full demonstration of the power of the government, and his stature as its representative. After General Atkinson had spoken of the mutual peace and friendship between the parties the Poncas "agreed to sign the document and then circulated a peace pipe. There were no real negotiations because the commissioners had already drawn up the treaty." [59] This second treaty was initiated by the government out of its desire to create a protocol for trade:

> All trade and intercourse with the Poncar tribe shall be transacted at such place or places as may be designated and pointed out by the President of the United States, through his agents; and none but American citizens, duly authorized by the United States, shall be admitted to trade or hold intercourse with said tribe of Indians. [60]

The Ponca Treaty of 1858. On March 12, 1858, six chiefs representing the Ponca tribe signed their third treaty in Washington D.C. The government was represented by Commissioner Charles E. Mix. The Poncas needed protection from Brule raids. They also needed food rations because of serious crop failures.[61]

Note: The two main divisions of the Sioux Tribe were the Eastern Sioux (Dakota/Santee) and the Western Sioux (Lakota). The Brule were one of seven sub-divisions of the Lakota.[62]

Facing starvation, the only thing the Poncas had left to bargain with was their land. The government acquired 96,000 acres from the Poncas in exchange for the following promises:

1) To protect their persons and property.

2) To make annuity payments staggered over 30 years.

3) To make a first-year payment of $20,000 to buy cattle and farming equipment, break up and fence the land, and build houses, "as may be necessary for their comfort and welfare."

4) To pay $5,000 per year for ten years to "build and maintain one or more manual-labor schools for the education and training of the Ponca youth in letters, agriculture, the mechanic arts, and housewifery."[63]

The Poncas were left with only 30,000 acres of land.[64] After this 1858 Treaty was signed, the Commissioner of Indian Affairs spoke of his real motive in treaty-making with the Poncas:

> Treaties were entered into...with the Poncas...for the purpose of extinguishing their title to all the lands occupied and claimed by them, except small portions on which to colonize and domesticate them.[65]

A major difference between the Ponca and American legal systems was in the timing of when promises made in the treaty would actually begin. The Poncas proceeded to carry out their treaty obligations shortly after the chiefs signed. Whereas, the government had to work through its slow procedural bureaucracy required by the Constitution from the time the treaty was signed by a representative of the President, followed by submission to the Senate for advice and consent. If it was approved by a two-thirds vote of the Senate, the House would assign the treaty to a committee to determine what funds would be appropriated. When this process was completed, allocated funds would trickle down to the Bureau Agents for ultimate delivery to the Poncas.

Soon after the Treaty of 1858 was signed, the Poncas moved from their land and abandoned their growing crops. They expected the government to protect them from Brule attacks and fulfill their treaty obligations. It did not. In the meantime, the Brule attacked them in late July 1859 killing their chief and others:

> Nearly all the Poncas' tipis were destroyed, their horses taken, their meat burned. The Brule even cut their moccasins into pieces ... (Agent) Gregory asked for two companies of troops to protect the Poncas and one thousand dollars' worth of food, guns and ammunition, but his request fell upon deaf ears. [66]

Government protection from the Brule attacks never came, in direct violation of Article 2. of the Treaty of 1858. Yet, the Poncas continued to remain faithful to their treaty obligations.

The Ponca Treaty of 1865. The Ponca chiefs signed their final treaty with the government on March 10, 1865. Meeting in Washington D.C., the government delegation was led by Commissioner William P. Dole. The Poncas ceded their remaining 30,000 acres to the government, and in exchange, the government returned the 96,000 acres it had acquired from the Poncas in the 1858 Treaty. The government said that it did this as a "way of rewarding them for their constant fidelity to the Government and citizens thereof, and with a view to returning to the said tribe of Ponca Indians their old burying grounds and corn fields."[67]

Unfortunately, Article 2. of the Treaty of 1865 contained the following unjust burden placed upon the Poncas:

> The United States shall not be called upon to satisfy or pay the claims of any settlers for improvements upon the lands above ceded to by the United States to the Poncas, but that the Ponca tribe of Indians shall, out of their own funds, and at their own expense, satisfy said claimants.[68]

The Government's Blunder

On April 29, 1868, the government signed the Fort Laramie Treaty with the Lakota Sioux. In exchange for peace, the government gave the Lakota the western half of South Dakota and, through a "clerical error" it gave the Lakotas the 96,000 acres previously given to the Poncas in 1865. So, within three years, the government had given the same land to two different tribes![69]

The 96,000 acres were taken from the Poncas by the government without the Poncas' consent or knowledge, in direct violation of the Ponca Treaty of 1865 and Article VI of the United States Constitution. The Poncas received no compensation for this act of injustice. Nebraska Historian Addison Sheldon called this tragic "error" cruel, saying:

> It took away from them their home, their gardens, and the graves of their fathers, which they had defended against the Sioux for hundreds of years and made a present of them to their deadly foes, the Sioux. Nothing so cruel or unjust was ever done by the United States to another tribe of Indians. And this was done to a tribe which was always the friend of the white men.... The Poncas had no place to go and remained upon their old reserve even though in daily danger from the Sioux.[70]

Twelve years later, the Senate Select Committee on the Removal of the Ponca Indians reported:

> The committee have been unable to discover any reason for thus including this reservation within the Sioux reservation and thus depriving the Poncas of the land that had been before granted to them by the United States with a solemn covenant of warranty. The Commissioner of Indian Affairs, in his report for the year 1878, describes it as a blunder, in the following words: "by a blunder in making the Sioux treaty of 1868, the 96,000 acres belonging to the Poncas were ceded to the Sioux. The negotiators had no right whatever to make the cession."[71]

Indian Appropriation Act of 1871

In 1871, Congress enacted the Indian Appropriation Act that stopped all treaty-making with Native American tribes, declaring:

> Hereafter no Indian nation or tribe within the territory of the United States shall be acknowledged or recognized as an independent nation, tribe or power with whom the United States may contract by treaty; but no obligation of any treaty lawfully made and ratified with any such Indian Nation or tribe prior to March 3, 1871, shall be hereby invalidated or impaired.[72]

Summary

Fifteen years after the last treaty with the Poncas was signed, a government report issued a strong defense of the Ponca tribe:

> In all accounts of the character of these Indians, and in all mention of them in official reports, they are described as among the most peaceful and quiet of all the Indians in the United States. Their disposition toward the United States has been uniformly friendly; they had never been known to cause trouble or disturbance, to make war upon the Indians or upon settlers. They cultivated the land, and many of them had farms of considerable size occupied in severalty, and altogether they presented one of the most encouraging and hopeful of all the fields for Indian improvement and self-support. [73]

The Poncas and other Native American tribes were at a distinct disadvantage during the treaty-making process because of their inability to speak or read English, and their misunderstandings of the interpreters' explanations. The government representatives wrote all of the treaties.[74]

**As treaty-making with the Poncas ended,
the process of displacement began.**

Chapter 6

Displacement

Ulysses S. Grant was sworn in as the 18th President of the United States in early 1869. He appointed William Tecumseh Sherman to be the General-in-Chief of the United States Army. Lieutenant General Philip Sheridan was placed in command of the military's Division of the Missouri, headquartered in Chicago. Within Sheridan's Division, Brigadier General George Crook was appointed as Commander of the Department of the Platte, headquartered at Fort Omaha. The military's presence in the Great Plains was now under the leadership of experienced civil war commanders.

The Vanishing Buffalo

At the same time, the buffalo herds, still a staple for many tribes in the Great Plains, were vanishing. Killing the buffalo with rifles became a popular "sport" leading to the useless slaughtering of thousands of these animals, their carcasses left to rot in the sun. The government did nothing to stop this slaughter. In fact, Secretary of the Interior Delano commented in 1874:

> The buffalo are disappearing rapidly, but not faster than I desire. I regard the destruction of such game as facilitating the policy of the government, of destroying their hunting habits, coercing them on reservations, and compelling them to begin to adopt the habits of civilization.[75]

General Sheridan also applauded the slaughter saying the white buffalo hunters "have done more in the last two years, and will do more in the next year, to settle the vexed Indian question, than the entire regular army has done in the last thirty years. They are destroying the Indian's commissary."[76]

It should be noted however, that "some military men, most notably General George Crook were known for their sincere concern for the Indians and their welfare."[77]

The inhumane slaughter of the buffalo caused terrible suffering for many of the Great Plains tribes who depended upon this special animal for its many uses vital to their survival. Ethnologist Alice C. Fletcher described the special songs and rituals that went into the annual buffalo hunt.[78] She said the slaughter of the buffalo also destroyed an event that had a unique social and religious dimension to it:

> The food on which their fathers had depended and which through past centuries had never failed, had been destroyed although they (the buffalo) had been sent from every quarter for man's use, by Wakonda. Distress of mind accompanied distress of body.[79]

With the disappearance of the buffalo herds and frequent attacks by the Brule, the Poncas were reaching a breaking point.[80] In 1873, a great flood further damaged their land. At some point, the Poncas expressed the possibility that they might be open to moving onto the Omaha tribe reservation, provided their cousins sold them land upon which to live and farm independently. Their openness to such a move, however, changed in the summer of 1876, when the Poncas signed a peace treaty with the Brule.[81]

Prior to that peace treaty, the August 12, 1874 edition of *The Bismarck Tribune*, a newspaper in Dakota Territory, confirmed General George A. Custer's report that he and a group of soldiers out on reconnaissance in the Black Hills had discovered "gold and silver in immense quantities."[82] The discovery was in a "mineral rich region of Western Dakota Territory that belonged to the Sioux Indians according to the Fort Laramie Treaty of 1868."[83]

The Sioux resolved to protect their land and way of life from this incursion. The Cheyenne joined them at the Battle of the Little Big Horn in June 1876, and defeated Custer's Seventh Cavalry Regiment. [84]

Government Reaction to Little Big Horn

In the spring of 1877, as a result of the defeat of Custer's Regiment and the public outcry that followed, the government responded with a decision to move the Northern Cheyennes to Indian Territory.[85]

At the same time, the government decided to move the Poncas to Indian Territory even though they had never broken a treaty, were friendly neighbors to white settlers, and had never taken up arms against the government. There was no justification for the government to move the Poncas, except for the fact that it could because the Poncas were small in number and defenseless.[86]

The Bureau of Indian Affairs sent Inspector Edward C. Kemble to visit the Poncas and begin the process of displacement.

Edward C. Kemble

Edward Cleveland Kemble was born in 1828 in Troy, New York. As a teenager, he traveled to California to work for newspapers as printer and editor. He served as a Sergeant in John C. Fremont's Bear Flag Revolt of 1846 against Mexico; and later mined for gold. He became a war correspondent for the Sacramento Union newspaper, and visited the Ponca village for the first time in 1862. He returned to observe the Poncas in 1872-73 as a representative of the Episcopal church, which often supplied them with food and clothing. In his testimony in 1880 before the Senate Select Committee, Kemble stated that he was a sponsor of some of the Ponca children at their baptisms at that time.[87]

Kemble Arrives at The Ponca Village

On January 26, 1877, Inspector Kemble arrived at the Ponca village to meet with their chiefs: Paramount Chief White Eagle, Standing Bear, Big Elk, Little Picker, Standing Buffalo, Sitting Bear, Little Chief, Smoke Maker, White Swan and Lone Chief.

Kemble informed the chiefs that the government had decided to move the Ponca tribe to Indian Territory, present-day Oklahoma.[88] The chiefs said they did not want to go. They wanted to stay on their own land. Standing Bear rose to speak on behalf of the chiefs, saying, "This is our land; we were born here. We have lived here all our lives till now. We are growing old here and we hope to die here."[89]

Inspector Kemble knew he had a difficult situation on his hands. He suggested the chiefs accompany him to Indian Territory to see the land reserved for them. He promised them that if they did not like it, they could meet with President Hayes at the White House. [90]

Chiefs Visit Indian Territory

On February 2, 1877 the Ponca Chiefs boarded the train with Kemble for the 500-mile journey to Indian Territory. They were accompanied by James Lawrence, Indian Affairs Agent, Charles LeClaire, Indian Affairs Interpreter, and Rev. Samuel D. Hinman, Episcopal minister.[91] Kemble said that he took the Reverend Hinman along because "he has known the Poncas ever since his tribe, the Santees, for which he is the missionary, have settled on the river."[92]

Seven days later the group arrived at the Osage village in Indian Territory. The Ponca chiefs immediately realized the land was not suitable for farming because it was dry, dusty and laden with rocks. The hard soil was not good for growing corn, wheat and potatoes. In addition, they could see that their cousins, the Osage and Kaw tribes, were sick and sad.[93] Chief White Eagle described what he saw when they reached Indian Territory:

> We were sick twice and we saw how the people of that land were, and we saw those stones and rocks and thought these two tribes (Osages and Kaws) were not able to do much for themselves.[94]

After visiting a few villages, the chiefs had enough. White Eagle spoke to Inspector Kemble.[95]

White Eagle:	Take me with you to see the Great Father. You said formerly we could tell him whatever we saw, good or bad, and I wish to tell him.
Kemble:	No, I don't wish to take you to see him.
White Eagle:	If you will not take me to the Great Father, take me home to my own country.
Kemble:	No, I'll not take you to your house. Walk there if you want.
White Eagle:	It makes my heart feel sad, as I do not know this land.

In the morning, Kemble and his group left the hotel and boarded a train for Dakota. Kemble had no intention of fulfilling his promise. He gave the chiefs two choices: accept the land offered to them in Indian Territory or walk home. The chiefs refused to stay, but without any money or passes for a train ride, and with no horses or wagons, they decided to walk home, with only blankets for warmth, and raw corn for food. By the time they arrived at the Omaha tribe village, they were barefoot, sick and exhausted.[96]

In testimony given by Bright Eyes on February 13, 1880 in Washington D.C. before the Senate Select Committee on the Ponca Removal, she gave a detailed description of her direct knowledge of the chiefs' story concerning what happened in Indian Territory and their journey to her village. She testified that her uncle, White Swan, who was one of the Ponca chiefs, stayed in her mother's home and told his story. Her father, Iron Eye, Chief of the Omaha Tribe, would had been there as well. Bright Eyes said that Standing Bear and the other chiefs:

> Came to my house and took dinner with me. They were all tired out and nearly sick. They were in really a pitiful condition. They stayed three or four days with me. Rev. Mr. Hamilton, our missionary, wrote down what they said; I was the interpreter. Several other Omaha's were present.[97]

After the chiefs shared their story with their cousins and were comforted, they left on the last leg of their journey home. But first they stopped in Sloan, Iowa on March 27, 1877 to send a telegram to President Rutherford B. Hayes. Bright Eyes said, "I wrote the telegram for the Poncas; Mr. Hamilton copied it."[98] The Chiefs asked the President a simple question:

> Did you authorize the man you sent to take us down to the Indian Territory to select a place for our future home, to leave us there to find our way back, as best we could, if we did not agree to go down there? This he told us, and left us without a pass, interpreter, or money, because we could not select one of three places, telling us if we did not go there peaceably, we would be driven by soldiers, at the point of the bayonet, from our present homes. We were so left and have been thirty days getting back as far as the Omahas, hungry, tired, shoeless, footsore and sad of heart. Please answer us at once, for we are in trouble.[99]

The telegram was signed by White Eagle, Standing Bear, Smoke Maker, Standing Buffalo, Frank LaFlesche, Little Chief, Big Elk, and Gahega.[100]

The President did not reply. In her testimony before the Senate Select Committee, Bright Eyes stated that she was told this fact by White Eagle and by her uncle White Swan.[101]

Standing Bear Arrested

The chiefs arrived back in their village on the Nebraska/Dakota border on April 2, 1877. Inspector Kemble was waiting for them with a government order to move the Poncas to Indian Territory. When the chiefs were informed of this order, they assembled in tribal council to decide how to respond. Standing Bear said they would not leave their land. He described what happened next:

> Then the soldiers came, and we locked our doors, and the women and children hid in the woods. Then the soldiers drove all the people the other side of the river, but my brother Big Snake and I. We did not go; and the soldiers took us and carried us away to a fort (Fort Randall) and put us in jail. There were eight officers who held council with us after we got there. They kept us in jail ten days. Then they carried us back to our home. The soldiers collected all the women and children together; then they called all the chiefs together in council; and then they took wagons and went round and broke open the houses. When we came back from the council, we found the women and children surrounded by a guard of soldiers. We told them we would rather die than leave our lands; but we could not help ourselves. They took us down.[102]

Summary

In 1880, the Senate Select Committee on the Removal of the Poncas issued a report in which it condemned this removal:

> The removal of a tribe of Indians who had always been in friendly relations to the government from their homes

> on a reservation confirmed to them by solemn treaty to a distant, and to them unknown, section of country, was a matter of great importance, and worthy the earnest consideration in all its details of the head of the department. The first duty under the law was manifestly to obtain in some authentic manner the consent of the tribe of Indians to be removed.[103]

The Senate Report also chastised Inspector Kemble and his superiors at the Department of the Interior for the manner in which the entire removal process was handled:

> Kemble was called to this duty, and apparently without any knowledge as to his fitness. His instructions from time to time evidenced a lack of appreciation on the part of the Department of the dignity and importance of his work. With this most important matter in the hands of a person totally unfitted for the work devolved upon him, accompanied by indifference and lack of knowledge upon the part of his superiors, what follows is not only not surprising, but entirely inevitable.... At no time did those representing the government ever frankly and fairly state to these Indians that they had the liberty of free choice to stay upon their own lands or to remove to the Indian Territory.[104]

Without weapons, these peaceful, honorable people had stood against the government with great courage and heartfelt resolve. But they were powerless against the soldiers called in to move them south.

Almost everything they possessed - their homes, their land, their farm implements, their way of life - was about to be taken from them.

Soon, what they had known and cherished would be gone.

Chapter 7

The Ponca Journey of Sorrows

Secretary of the Interior Carl Schurz replaced Inspector Kemble with E. A. Howard who held one last meeting with the Ponca chiefs on May 15, 1877. After four hours of unsuccessful talks, he sent for forty soldiers from the Army's Infantry and Cavalry stationed at Fort Sully and Fort Randall to carry out the order for removal.[105]

At this time, the Ponca tribe numbered 710[106] (*Note:* Just three years earlier their population was 733, with Standing Bear's band consisting of 82 people). The Poncas left their home in two parties. The first party consisted of Lone Chief and 170 members of the Ponca tribe who left on April 17, 1877 for Indian Territory, escorted by Inspector Lawrence and a small group of soldiers. Kemble joined them later and was with them when they arrived at the Quapaw reservation on June 12, 1877. The second group of Poncas, consisting of 540 men, women and children, including Standing Bear, left their ancestral homeland on May 16, 1877, escorted by Major Walker and 25 soldiers. They were joined by Inspector E. A. Howard.[107]

The Poncas were told to take everything they owned to the Indian Agency building before they left their homes. Thomas H. Tibbles, deputy editor for the *Omaha Herald* newspaper interviewed Standing Bear a few years later about what happened next. Standing Bear told Tibbles that it took him three days to comply with the government order because he had accumulated so much property. Proud of his hard work, yet deeply sad and disheartened, Standing Bear described the property the government took from him:

> One house (I built it with my own hands. It took me a long time for I didn't know how very well). It was twenty feet by forty feet, with two rooms, three lamps, four chairs, one table, two new bedstands, two washtubs and washboard, two new cooking stoves, one heating stove, two trunks (one very large), one valise, crockery, knives and forks. I also had four cows, three steers, eight horses, four hogs, five wagon-loads of corn with the side-boards on (about 130 bushels), one hundred sacks of wheat, and one wagon-load loose, which I had in boxes (about 275 bushels), twenty-one chickens, two turkeys, one prairie breaking plow, two stirring plows, a good stable and cattle sheds, three axes, two hatchets, one saw, three pitchforks, five plows, a good stable and cattle sheds, one cross-cut saw, two log chains, two ox-yokes, two ladders, and a great many other things which I cannot now remember. These things were mine. I had worked for them all. By their order, I brought them all, except the house and such things as I could not move, to the Agency, and they put them in a big house and locked them up. I have never seen any of them since. Our wagons and ponies they did not take away.[108]

In his testimony before the Senate Select Committee, Thomas Tibbles reported what he saw during his on-site visit to the Ponca villages in the fall of 1879:

> The Ponca tribe consists of two bands: the one under White Eagle lived on the Niobrara River; the one under Standing Bear lived on the Missouri River. The Agency building, sawmill, blacksmith shop, etc. were on the Missouri River village. They were five miles apart. 29 houses were still standing. Part of Standing Bear' house was torn down to within four feet of the foundation, and all the materials of the upper part carried away. On the Niobrara side all the houses were torn down.[109]

Paramount Chief White Eagle confirmed Tibbles testimony saying that after the Poncas had left their Niobrara village, the soldiers tore down all of their log homes which the Poncas had built themselves mostly from logs or sawed lumber from the tribe's sawmill. The soldiers also tore down all their barns, cattle sheds, tribal grist mill, sawmill, schoolhouse and their church. The blacksmith shop and the Indian Agency building were left standing. Some fifty cooking stoves were broken into pieces. The logs from their homes were thrown into piles for auction. [110]

It must have looked like a tornado had ripped through the Ponca villages. Almost everything was gone; destroyed for no reason.

Chief White Eagle described how the women and children greatly feared the soldiers when they began the forced march:

> They forced us across the Niobrara to the other side, just as one would drive a herd of ponies; and the soldiers pushed us on until we came to the Platte River. They drove us on in advance just as if we were a herd of ponies.[111]

Howard's Diary of the Journey

Inspector E. A. Howard, the government representative who accompanied Standing Bear's group of Poncas and the soldiers on the journey to Indian Territory, kept a "Journal of the March." This Journal was included in *The Annual Report* given by E.A. Hayt, Commissioner for Indian Affairs, to the Secretary of the Interior for the year 1877. Excerpts from this Journal convey the terrible suffering and utter horrors endured by the Ponca people.[112]

> *May 16.* They [the Chiefs] sent word to me at an early hour that they had considered my words and had concluded to go with me, and that they wanted assistance in getting the old and infirm over the Niobrara River which was much swollen by the rains and at a low

temperature....At five o'clock PM had the entire tribe with their effects across the river, off the reservation, and in camp in Nebraska....The current so swift that it was found impossible to move the goods across in any other way than by packing them on the shoulders of the men, the quicksand bottom rendering it unsafe to trust them on the backs of animals.

May 19. A severe thunderstorm occurred during the night of the 16th and heavy rains prevailed during the day and night of the 17th, rendering it impossible to make any further preparations for breaking camp....For two or three hours before daybreak on the 19th it rained heavily....But at ten o'clock I gave orders to break camp....During the day an Indian child died.

May 23. The morning opened with light rain, but at eight o'clock a terrific thunderstorm occurred of two hours' duration, which was followed by steady rain throughout the day, in consequence of which we remained in camp. During the day a child died.

May 24. Buried the child that died yesterday in the cemetery at Neligh, giving it a Christian burial.

Note: At the brief burial service for White Buffalo Girl, her father made a heartfelt plea to the people of Neligh to take care of the grave of his eighteen-month-old child as they would one of their own. The people of Neligh have honored his wishes to this day with flowers and toys laid at her tomb.[113]

May 27. The morning opened cold, with a misty rain.... Broke camp at eight and marched eight miles further down Shell Creek, when a heavy thunderstorm coming on, we again went into camp. Several of the Indians were here found to be quite sick, and having no physician, and none being attainable, they gave us much anxiety and no little trouble. The daughter of Standing Bear, one of the chiefs, was very low of consumption, and moving her with any degree of comfort was almost impossible, and the same trouble existed in transporting all the sick.

May 28. Last evening, I gave orders to break camp at 5:00 this morning, intending, if practicable, to reach Columbus before night, but a heavy thunderstorm prevailed at that hour.

Note: Bright Eyes said her uncle White Swan, one of the Ponca Chiefs, sent word to the Omahas that they should meet the Poncas near Columbus, Nebraska to say goodbye since they may never see their cousins again. She along with her father, Chief Iron Eye, and eight other Omahas rode over - "we met them on the road; they were all crying. I heard men crying all night."[114]

June 6. Prairie Flower, wife of Shines White, and daughter of Standing Bear, who died yesterday, was given Christian burial, her remains being deposited in the cemetery at Milford, Nebraska, a small village on the Blue River. Quite a heavy rain during the afternoon. The storm, the most disastrous of any that occurred during the removal of the Poncas under my charge, came suddenly upon us while in camp on the evening of this day. It was a storm such as I never before experienced....The wind blew a fearful tornado, demolishing every tent in camp, and rending many of them into shreds, overturning wagons, and hurling wagon-boxes, camp-equipages, etc. through the air in every direction like straws. Some of the people were taken up by the wind and carried as much as three hundred yards. Several of the Indians were quite seriously hurt, and one child died the next day from injuries received.

June 9. Put the child that died yesterday in the coffin and sent it back to Milford, to be buried in the same grave with its aunt, Prairie Flower.

> *June 16.* Reached Marysville, Kansas where we went into camp. During the march a wagon tipped over injuring a woman severely. Indians out of rations and feeling hostile.
>
> *June 18.* Little Cottonwood died. Four families determined to return to Dakota. I was obliged to ride 9 miles on horseback to overtake them to restore harmony and settle difficulty in camp. Had coffin made for dead Indians. A fearful thunderstorm during the night, flooding the camp equipage.
>
> *June 25.* Two old women died during the day.
>
> *July 9.* Broke camp at six o'clock, passing through Baxter Springs at about one o'clock. Just after passing Box Springs, and between that place and the reservation, a terrible thunderstorm struck us. The wind blew a heavy gale and the rain fell in torrents, so that it was impossible to see more than four or five rods distant, thoroughly drenching every person and every article; making a fitting ending to a journey commenced by wading a river and thereafter encountering innumerable storms.

In his final journal entry Howard wrote:

> During the last few days of the journey the weather was exceedingly hot, and the teams terribly annoyed and bitten by green-head flies, which attacked them in great numbers. Many of the teams were nearly exhausted and had the distance been a little farther, they must have given out. The people were all nearly worn out from the fatigue of the march.[115]

Howard recorded in his Journal the deaths of nine members of the Ponca Tribe during the course of the 55-day march: five children, two young adults, and two elderly women.

Howard was with the Poncas for a few days before the removal and remained with them in Indian Territory for a while. He then left them to fend for themselves, writing:

> I am of the opinion that the removal of the Poncas from the northern climate of Dakota to the southern climate of the Indian Territory, at the season of the year it was done, will prove a mistake, and that a great mortality will surely follow among the people when they shall have been here for a time and become poisoned with the malaria of the climate. It is a matter of astonishment to me that the government should have ordered the removal of the Ponca Indians to Indian Territory without having first made some provision for their settlement and comfort. As the case now is, no appropriation has been made by Congress; no houses have been built for their use, and the result is that these people have been placed on an uncultivated reservation to live in their tents as best they may.[116]

Howard also acknowledged that the Poncas had not consented to the removal and in fact, he said:

> The title to the old Ponca reservation in Dakota still remains in the Poncas, they having signed no papers relinquishing their title nor having violated any of the provisions of the treaty by which it was ceded to them by the government.[117]

A few years later, Standing Bear described what happened upon arrival in Indian Territory:

> In our own land we lived in houses made of wood that kept out snow and rain and kept us warm in winter. Many of us had two stoves each to keep the house warm, but when we went down there we had to live in tents that let the rain and snow get in, and we had no stoves; and so a great many of my people got sick and died.[118]

The Senate Select Committee on the Removal of the Poncas in 1880 stated in its report:

> The Tribe was taken to the Indian Territory without any previous arrangement for their permanent location there. They were temporarily located near Baxter Springs, on the Quapaw reservation and lived in canvas tents during the winter.... They became exceedingly home-sick and discontented, which aggravated greatly the evils under which they were suffering.[119]

The Ponca Journey of Sorrows

May 16, 1877 to July 9, 1877

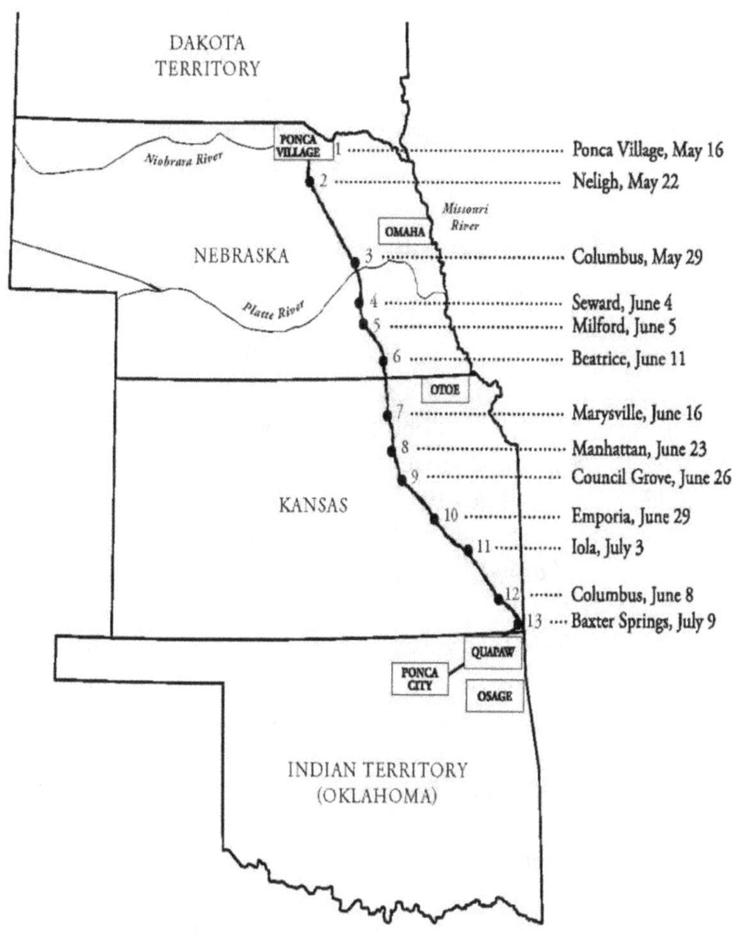

Source of locations and dates:
E. A. Howard's "Journal of the March"

Ponca Chiefs Meet President Hayes

Secretary Carl Schurz, upon the recommendation of the new Indian Commissioner E.A. Hayt, granted the request of Paramount Chief White Eagle and Chief Standing Bear to visit the President. They and other Ponca chiefs boarded a train to Washington D.C. and met with President Rutherford B. Hayes in early November 1877. The President told them to remain in Indian Territory and assured them the government would take better care of them.[120]

Chiefs Return to Indian Territory

When the chiefs returned to Indian Territory, they found their people in worse condition than when they had left. Standing Bear's grandmother, sister, and mother-in-law died of fever and malnutrition. The Poncas had no means to support themselves. In less than 18 months since their removal, a total of 158 of the original 710 members of the tribe died of pneumonia, malaria or malnutrition. Nearly one-fourth of the tribe was dead, just as Inspector E.A. Howard had predicted [121]

At two different government hearings, Chief White Eagle described what he saw when he returned: "Every person and animal was sick or dying. We were as grass that is trodden down."[122] One committee member asked the Chief a very direct question to which White Eagle gave just as direct an answer:

Committee:	Why do you not cultivate land down there?
White Eagle:	Our ponies died of disease; and our cattle died; and then we had no plows. That is the reason."[123]

In 1881, the government issued a very blunt assessment of its handling of this matter:

> This failure had involved the government in a transaction which can find no justification. It has led the government to

violate in dealing with one of the most peaceable, orderly and well-disposed of all the tribes of Indians, in the most flagrant manner, their rights of property, to disregard their appeals to the honor and justice of the United States, and the dictates of humanity. The Committee can find no language sufficiently strong in which to condemn the whole proceedings and trace to it all the troubles which have come upon the Poncas, and the hardships and sufferings which have followed them since they were taken by the United States from their old reservation and placed in their present location in the Indian Territory.[124]

Ponca delegation meets President Hayes,
Washington D.C., November 1877
Back row: John Barnaby and Charles H. LeClaire (interpreters.)
Front row (left to right): Standing Bear, Paramount Chief White Eagle, Standing Buffalo, Big Elk
Courtesy of History Nebraska, RG2066-04-02-1

Where Could the Poncas Turn for Help?

The Poncas had no legal rights in any United States Court to file a petition for a redress of grievances or crimes committed against them because the American legal system considered them merely "wards of the government," not persons.[125]

The Poncas could be arrested at any time for leaving their reservation in Indian Territory without government permission.

The government, at any time, could and did take away their land, homes, farm equipment, threshing machines, reapers, crops, buildings and household furniture, without compensation or justification.

Sickness and death were their constant companion. The Poncas hope for survival, was gone. Something must be done.

Someone must take action.

Chapter 8

Standing Bear Takes Action

In December 1878, Standing Bear's teenage son, Bear Shield, died. Standing Bear had already lost his daughter Prairie Flower and other members of his family in the past 18 months. But the death of his son must have been especially hard on him because it was "usually the son of a chief who took his father's place when the old man died." [126]

Bear Shield's final request to his father was to be buried alongside the bones of his ancestors in his homeland. It was a tradition that if a Ponca was not buried with the bones of his ancestors, he would wander the next world alone. Family and tradition meant everything to the Poncas. Standing Bear was a loving father so, he promised his son he would take him home and bury him in the ancestral burial grounds of his people. Months later, Standing Bear reflected back on that decision to go home:

> I was in an awful place, and I was a prisoner there. I was not a free man. I had been taken by force from my own country to a strange land and was a captive. I could see nothing ahead but death for the whole tribe. I was much sorry for the little children who were so very sick. They would moan and moan, and we had no medicine and no way to help them. I said I will take a small party and start back to my old home. If the soldiers come after us I will not fight. Whatever they do, it can't be worse than to stay here. [127]

The Quest for Freedom Begins

On January 2, 1879, facing hunger, sickness and death, with no recognized standing to file a action in any American court for protection or redress of grievances, Standing Bear left Indian Territory. Twenty-nine men, women and children left with him, including his two grandchildren from his daughter Prairie Flower. He carried with him the bones of his beloved son, Bear Shield. These courageous Poncas led by Standing Bear left with a few wagons and a few horses on a 500 mile walk home in below-zero weather. After 20 days, their money and food were gone. [128]

Enduring cold, ice, hunger, thirst, sickness, fear and worry of the unknown, they must have wondered what they would face when they got home – if they ever reached home. The likelihood of some or all of them dying on the journey was real. They may not have survived the journey but for the kindness of some white farmers along the way.

Standing Bear recalled that "the white people treated us very kindly; some gave us bread, some coffee, and others meal or flour; none of them refused to give us anything when they saw we were hungry."[129] Such acts of kindness, together with Ponca resolve, allowed them to finish their journey home. But what would await them?

March 4, 1879

Sixty-two days into their journey, Standing Bear and his companions arrived near the village of the Omaha tribe, March 4, 1879. Chief Iron Eye (Joseph LaFlesche), Bright Eyes (Susette LaFlesche) and a few others heard of their arrival and went to greet them. They were shocked at what they saw. The Poncas were starving from malnutrition, their feet were bleeding, and frostbite had blackened their skin. The Omahas tended to their every need and listened to them share their sad journey. Iron Eye gave them some land and seed so they could reclaim their lifestyle and become self-supporting again. The Omahas did everything they could to help the Poncas regain self-esteem.

On the day the Poncas arrived at the Omaha reservation, Jacob Vore, Indian Agent to the Omaha tribe, sent a telegram to the office of Carl Schurz, Secretary of the Interior informing him that "the Poncas have just arrived thirty in number; had them arrested, they promise to remain for orders, have no place to confine them. I await instructions." Secretary Schurz then sent an order by telegram to George W. McCray, Secretary of War saying, "the nearest military commander be instructed to detail a sufficient guard to return these Poncas to the agency where they belong."[130]

McCray set the process in motion. First, he transmitted Schurz's letter to General Sherman on March 14th, who in turn forwarded the message to General Sheridan on March 17th. Two days later, General George Crook, Commanding General of the Department of the Platte, stationed at Fort Omaha, Nebraska, received his orders from Sheridan.

General Crook directed John H. King, Commander of the 9th Infantry and Post Commander at Fort Omaha, to send a detachment to the Omaha tribal village near Decatur, Nebraska, to arrest the Poncas and escort them back to Fort Omaha.

Poncas Arrested

William L. Carpenter, First Lieutenant of the 9th Infantry, together with a corporal and five enlisted men, using three saddle horses and a military ambulance drawn by four mules, was dispatched to the Omaha village. On March 23, 1879, the soldiers arrested Standing Bear and the 29 Poncas. Two of the Poncas were not well enough to travel and were allowed to remain on the Omaha tribe reservation. Standing Bear described the scene:

> When we started back the scene among the women and children was heart-rending. They and their friends among the Omahas cried most bitterly. It would break one's

> heart to look at them. Many were still sick, and all felt that we were going back to certain death. My efforts to save their lives had failed.[131]

Bright Eyes was a witness to the heartbreaking arrest and feared the soldiers were taking the Poncas directly back to Indian Territory:

> We were all formerly one people, the same as brothers.... Standing Bear said it was no use to resist, they had committed no crime, had done no wrong, but the government was strong, and they were powerless and could not resist. The next morning the soldiers started off with them; we were standing by the door and saw the whole company file past, as the soldiers were taking Standing Bear and his companions down to the Indian Territory. The Omahas felt very bad; but they could not even go and shake hands with them.[132]

Iron Eye (Joseph LaFlesche) Chief of Omaha Tribe
Father of Bright Eyes (1854)
Courtesy of History Nebraska RG2026-01

Chapter 9

Imprisoned at Fort Omaha

On March 25, 1879, the soldiers arrived at Fort Omaha with their prisoners. The Poncas were encamped in three temporary tent lodges near the entrance to the Fort. They would remain there for 55 days.

Fort Omaha and the Department of the Platte

In 1868, the government built a fort on 60 acres, four miles north of Omaha, Nebraska. It was named Sherman Barracks in honor of General William Tecumseh Sherman. It was updated and renamed Fort Omaha ten years later. A modern home was added in 1878 for the Commanding General, but not occupied by the Crooks until the fall of 1879.[133] Former President U.S. Grant and his wife visited the Crooks in November 1879 and stayed in their home for three days. In September 1880, President Rutherford B. Hayes dined at their home.[134]

Note: Today, the "Crook House" is open to the public and serves as headquarters of the Douglas County Historical Society.[135]

The Department of the Platte was created in 1866 as a military district to include present-day Iowa, Nebraska, Wyoming, Utah, and parts of Montana and Idaho. It was responsible for 14 supply and administration posts in that territory and it coordinated campaigns against various Northern tribes. When General Crook became Commander, he moved the department headquarters from the S.W. Corner of 15th Harney Street in downtown Omaha, to Fort Omaha.[136]

Staff Officers of the Department of the Platte, 1878-79
General Crook (seated front row middle),
Judge Advocate Horace B. Burnham (seated front row far right),
Lieutenant John G. Bourke, Aide-de-Camp to General Crook & reporter at Crook Interview of Ponca Prisoners (standing third from left). *Courtesy of Douglas County Historical Society*

George Crook

General George Crook was born on September 8, 1828, in Dayton, Ohio. He graduated from West Point in 1852 finishing 38th in a class of 43 cadets. Crook fought in Civil War battles at Manassas, Antietam and Chickamauga, and was present at Appomattox Courthouse when Lee surrendered to Grant. He served in the Western theater of operations after the war. Crook was appointed Commander of the Department of the Platte and moved to Omaha in 1875. His photographs proudly display his forked beard and unusual hats he liked to wear when not in uniform. He was an avid hunter and taxidermist. At the time of the Standing Bear trial, he was 50 years of age.[137] [138]

Iron Eye and Bright Eyes Visit Crook

The Poncas and Omahas were cousins. They came together to the Nebraska/Dakota region a few hundred years earlier. They lived near each other, and often intermarried. Chief Iron Eye and his daughter Bright Eyes were very close to their cousins. When they heard the Poncas were being led down to Indian Territory in May 1877, they went to see them and say goodbye.

Now, in March 1879, with the arrest of their cousins and an immanent move back to Indian Territory where they likely faced death, Iron Eye, Bright Eyes and the rest of the Omaha tribe were awakened to the terrible injustice that was done to the Ponca people over the past two years. The Omahas must have realized what the government had done to their peaceful cousins, it could also do to them. Ethnologist Alice C. Fletcher confirmed their fears when she wrote:

> Suddenly, in 1877, like a bolt out of the blue sky, came the distressing removal of their kindred, the Poncas, from their home on the Niobrara River to the Indian Territory. The pathetic return in the spring of 1879 of Standing Bear and his followers, bearing the bones of that chief's dearly loved son for burial, and the coming of United States soldiers to carry them back to the dreaded "hot country," brought terror to every Omaha family, thinking that their own homes might be in danger...and that even the government which they had always respected had betrayed them.[139]

So, two days after Standing Bear was arrested, Iron Eye and Bright Eyes rode their horses to Fort Omaha from their reservation near Decatur, Nebraska. They left their reservation without government permission, understanding the government could arrest them at any time. They were desperate to get help for their cousins. They felt General Crook needed to hear the full story of the suffering and deaths the Poncas endured in Indian Territory, and why Standing Bear and his companions made their journey in the midst of winter to come home.

General Crook was so disturbed by what he heard from Iron Eye and Bright Eyes that he decided he needed to speak with Thomas Tibbles, deputy editor of the *Omaha Herald* newspaper. Ordinarily, this would be a very unusual act on the part of the arresting officer. However, just two years earlier, General Crook had secretly enlisted the help of Tibbles with Spotted Tail, Chief of the Brule, concerning another government order Crook did not agree with.[140]

Thomas H. Tibbles

Thomas Henry Tibbles was born on May 22, 1840 near Athens, Ohio. He led a very colorful life before and after this story. At a young age, he left home to become an assistant to General James Lane in the fight against slavery in Kansas. At that time, he met abolitionist John Brown and narrowly escaped being hanged by a mob of pro-slavery men. He served as a scout and newspaper reporter during the Civil War. For a time, he lived with the Omaha Tribe. He learned their language and was initiated into the Soldiers Lodge, an honorary recognition by the tribe because of his common bond with them. George Crook was also a member of the Soldiers Lodge.[141] After the war, Tibbles became a circuit preacher for the Episcopal church. Wolfe's City of Omaha Directory for 1878-1879 identifies him as "Rev. T. Henry Tibbles."[142] In 1871, Tibbles became a reporter for an Omaha newspaper. At the time of the trial, he was 39 years of age. [143]

The Midnight Ride

On March 30, 1879, shortly after midnight, Crook took Iron Eye and Bright Eyes with him on a four-mile ride to the office of the *Omaha Herald* at 257 Farnam Street in Omaha.[144] It was 1:00 AM when they arrived. For the next three and one-half hours, Iron Eye and Bright Eyes told the Ponca story to Tibbles. At 4:30 AM, the meeting ended. General Crook told Tibbles that the fate of Standing Bear and his people was now in Tibbles hands.[145] [146]

Thomas H. Tibbles in 1900
Deputy Editor of the *Omaha Herald* at Time of the Trial
Courtesy of History Nebraska RG2737-04

Office of Thomas H. Tibbles, Omaha Herald Newspaper
(Daily/Weekly), Second floor above billiard saloon, 13th & Douglas Streets, Omaha, (Newspaper employees leaning out of the windows)
Courtesy from The Bostwick-Frohardt Collection owned by KM3TV and on permanent loan to The Durham Museum, Omaha. BF14-275

Chapter 10

Prisoners Interviewed

After only a few hours' sleep, Tibbles awoke knowing he needed to speak with Standing Bear. He wanted to confirm the story he heard from General Crook, Chief Iron Eye and Bright Eyes. He walked the four miles to Fort Omaha in about an hour on Sunday morning March 30, 1879, to interview Standing Bear and some of the other prisoners.[147]

Tibbles Interviews the Prisoners

The interview Tibbles had with the Ponca prisoners was reported in the April 1, 1879 morning edition of the *Omaha Herald.* Tibbles entered the tents where the Poncas were held prisoners. Charles Morgan was the interpreter. The first to speak was Buffalo Chip (Ta-zha-but). Tibbles said, "he spoke, talking slowly, and making emphatic gestures occasionally, as follows":

> When I was young, the gun was the greatest friend the Indian had...The gun is not my friend now. The greatest friend I have is the plow. The game *(buffalo)* is gone never to come back. I look everywhere and I see none. It has vanished away like a dream when I wake from sleep. But the ground is here. It can never vanish away. From the ground the Indian must live.... We talked among ourselves years ago. We agreed that we would raise cattle, horses, pigs and all kinds of stock. We said we would learn to plow, we would build houses out of wood, we would learn to do like the white people.... We told the men the Great Father sent to talk to us that we would do this years ago. We have kept our word. We have taught our hands to hold the plow handles. We built houses. We raised stock. Now look at us today. See these rags. We

> have no houses, no stock, no grain, we are prisoners in this camp, and we have never committed any crime.[148]

When Buffalo Chip stopped speaking, Tibbles waited patiently. After a period of silence, Buffalo Chip resumed speaking:

> Eight days ago, I was at work on my farm which the Omaha's gave me. I had sowed some spring wheat and wished to sow some more. I was living peaceably with all men. I have never committed any crime. I was arrested and brought back as a prisoner. Does your law do that? I have been told since the great war that all men were free men, and that no man can be made a prisoner unless he does wrong. I have done no wrong, and yet I am here a prisoner. Have you a law for white men and a different law for those who are not white? [149]

Tibbles noticed that "a feeling of solemnity came over all; they seemed to think death was very near in any event." Tibbles was especially moved by the sight of a young woman sitting in the back of the Lodge holding a baby close to herself, rocking "back and forth with tears running down over her face."[150]

Again, a period of silence came over the room. Then Charles Morgan, an interpreter for the Omaha Tribe, turned to Tibbles and said, "This is awful. These men are my friends. They are of my blood."[151]

Tibbles asked Buffalo Chip what should be done "in reference to the Indians and how the government should deal with them?" Buffalo Chip replied:

> It seems to me that the government should let the Indians go on some land that is good, where good crops could be raised. This land should be given them for theirs forever, given so the government could not take it away, so that the white men could not get it. Indians cannot make plows and axes and wagons, so the government

> should give them some to help them start. And they can't plow where the ground is all hills and stones like it is down where the Ponca reservation is.[152]

At this point in the interview, Buffalo Chip suggested:

> There should be laws to govern the Indians the same as the whites. A court should be established where those who do wrong, both Indians and white men, should be tried. We have never had a court. If white men steal our ponies, there is nobody to punish them. If the Indians do wrong, they make the tribe responsible and the soldiers come out and kill our people. We want land which shall be our own and we want a court. Let those who do right be protected and those who do wrong be punished.[153]

When Buffalo Chip finished speaking, Standing Bear decided to speak to Tibbles. He explained the horrors his people endured while living in Indian Territory:

> The first four months we were there, Agent Howard never issued us a pound of rations. We were all nearly starved to death.... Starvation so reduced our strength that when the sickness came on in the fall they could not stand it, and our people began to die. It was like a great house with a big fire in it, and everything was poison. We never saw such sickness before. One hundred and fifty of our people have died and more are dying every day...It is the worst country in the world. It was a place made to die in and not to live in. There is no land there which will raise anything, and we have nothing to farm with, for they never brought us the things they took away.[154]

Standing Bear also told the reporter of his personal tragedies and the reason he decided to make the journey home:

> My son died, my sister died and my brother there was near dying. We had nothing to do but sit still, be sick, starve and die. My son who died was a good boy, I did

> everything I could to help educate him, that when I was gone, he could live like the white men and teach these little ones (pointing to some little children). I am too old to learn to read and write and speak English....My boy who died down there, as he was dying looked up to me and said, I would like you to take my bones back and bury them there where I was born. I promised him I would. I could not refuse the dying words of my boy. I have attempted to keep my word. His bones are in that trunk.[155]

Near the end of the interview, Standing Bear's wife, Susette Primo, motioned to speak. "With eyes full of tears," she said:

> My mother is buried there, my grandmother and another child. My boy was a good boy and we tried to do what he wanted us to do. We were just getting ready to bury him when the soldiers came upon us. Won't you go to General Crook and ask him if we must go back south, to let us have time to take him back to the Agency and bury him? My heart is broken. My eyes are full of tears all the time, and ever since I came to this place there is an ache here (laying her hand on her heart). If we must go back, these little children will soon die too.[156]

After Standing Bear's wife spoke, Tibbles reported "such a feeling of depression and utter hopelessness settled down overall, that the Herald representative arose and left the lodge and walked around outside a few moments." When he returned, Standing Bear said that "we want to be under the same law as the white men. We want to be free."[157]

Tibbles' interview with the Ponca prisoners lasted for three hours. He realized he needed a plan to inform as many influential people as possible. The Poncas story had to be told quickly.

Omaha Clergy Send Telegram

Later that Sunday morning, Tibbles decided his first move would be to contact as many churches in Omaha as he could. He said that "he reached the Presbyterian church, Rev. Mr. Harsha pastor, just in time, and obtained permission to speak after the sermon. He then went to the Congregational Church, Rev. Mr. Sherrill pastor, and spoke between the opening hymns."[158] Tibbles asked each pastor to sign a resolution requesting the Secretary of the Interior to rescind the removal order so that General Crook could release the prisoners. Tibbles reported that "Rev. Mr. Jameson, who was an old friend and acquaintance of Mr. Schurz, wrote the following, which was signed and sent by telegram:[159]

Telegram to Secretary Carl Schurz

Omaha, Neb. March 31,1879

To Hon. Carl Schurz, Secretary of the Interior, Washington:

Seven lodges of Ponca Indians, who had settled on Omaha reservation, and were commencing to work at farming, have, by your order, been arrested to be taken south. I beseech you as a friend to have this order revoked. Several churches and congregations have passed resolutions recommending that these Indians be permitted to remain with the Omahas. Some of the Indians are too sick to travel. Particulars by mail.

E.H.E. Jameson, Pastor Baptist Church
H.D. Fisher, Pastor Methodist Church
W.J. Harsha, Pastor Presbyterian Church
A.F. Sherrill, Pastor Congregational Church

Tibbles arrived home about 11:00 PM. After eating a quick supper, he transcribed the notes of his interview with the Ponca prisoners. It took him six hours. After a few hours of sleep, he returned to Fort Omaha for a most unusual meeting.[160]

General Crook Interviews the Prisoners

On Monday, March 31, 1879, General Crook met with Standing Bear and other Poncas. He offered them an opportunity to present their story. Tibbles reported the interview in the April 1, 1879, edition of the *Omaha Herald.* In addition, Lieutenant John G. Bourke, aide-de-camp to General Crook, kept a diary for nearly 25 years beginning at West Point and ending in 1896. Bourke reported the interview in his diary.[161]

Note: Bourke's Diary is in important source of primary information for Ponca history. John Gregory Bourke (1846-1896) was a graduate of West Point (1869), a Medal of Honor recipient, an accomplished linguist (e.g., Latin, Greek, Gaelic, Apache) and a writer of ethnological studies. He married Mary Horbach of Omaha (1883) and they are buried in Arlington National Cemetery.

The interview took place in General Crook's office at Fort Omaha. It began at Noon and lasted two hours. It was unusual that the Commanding General of the United States Department of the Platte, the arresting officer, would meet in a non-judicial setting with his prisoners, considered under the law to be "wards of the government." Bourke reported 17 people were present at the meeting, including:

- ◊ Seven representatives of the military: Brigadier General George Crook, Lieut-col. Robert Williams, Ass't Adjt Genl. Lieut-col. Wm. B. Royall, Inspector General, Colonel M.I. Ludington, Chief Qr. Master, General John H. King, Col 9th Infantry, Captain A.S. Burt, 9th Infantry, and Lieut. John G. Bourke, 3 Cavalry, A.D.C;

- ◊ Eight members of the Ponca Tribe: Buffalo Chip, Cries for War, Yellow Horse, Long Runner, Crazy Bear, Buffalo Track, Little Duck, and Standing Bear;

- ◊ Charles Morgan, a member of the Omaha Tribe, interpreter;

◊ Thomas Tibbles, reporter and deputy editor of the *Omaha Herald*, only civilian present.[162]

Before recording the interview, Bourke wrote a description of Standing Bear in his diary saying that he was:

> A noble-looking Indian, tall and commanding in presence, dignified in manner and very elegantly dressed in the costume of his tribe. He wore a shirt made of blue flannel, having collar and cuffs of red cloth, ornamented with brass buttons, leggings of blue flannel, moccasins of deer-skin, and over his shoulders was draped a beautiful blanket, one-half red, the other half blue, with the lines of suture covered by a broad band of beadwork. The most striking feature in his attire was a necklace of claws of the grizzly bear of which he appeared highly proud.[163]

General Crook and the officers shook hands with the Poncas, who "then squatted in a semi-circle on the floor." General Crook informed Charles Morgan that the chiefs could begin speaking.[164]

General George Crook
Commander of the Department of the Platte
at Fort Omaha, in full uniform and forked beard, 1879
Courtesy of the Douglas County Historical Society

Standing Bear stood up and shook hands with General Crook for a second time. He then addressed him and the other officers with words of friendship, not anger, sharing a brief history of his people:

> We have come back from the ocean, the great water to the East ... and we have traveled until we have got to Dacotah Territ. A good many of our tribe have lived there on that old reservation. Somebody came there to our reservation and took us to another reservation. I had built my house with my own hand, broke the land, had horses and cattle. Then somebody else came there and threw my things away.[165]

After describing the sufferings and deaths of the two years the Poncas lived in Indian Territory, Standing Bear made his plea:

> My brothers, it just seems this way to me; as if a big prairie-fire was coming towards me: I would take hold of my wife and baby boy and run with them to a safe place. As if the Great River was overflowing, I'd try to get them up on the hills, out of danger. The Almighty has looked down upon me. He knows what I am saying. I think he has given me reason to say these words. I hope the Almighty may send a good spirit to my brothers and make them think of me... Oh, my brothers and my friends outside! I want you to look at me and take pity on me and help me to save my women and children. I need help.[166]

General Crook asked Charles Morgan a question or two and then responded to Standing Bear's plea, "I think myself it is a very hard case – but it is something I haven't anything to do with. I must obey my orders from Washington. We will give them plenty to eat while they are here. I know it's very hard and painful for them to go down and it's just as hard and painful for us to have to send them there."[167]

Lieutenant Bourke ended his diary entry for March 31, 1879, reporting that the meeting concluded with more handshaking.[168]

George Crook was a powerful force in this story. Standing Bear and the Poncas would have been sent back to Indian Territory without a trial had it not been for General Crook. He was willing to meet with Chief Iron Eye and Bright Eyes to hear them relate the plight of the Poncas. Then he took Iron Eye and Bright Eyes to the office of Thomas Tibbles at 1:00 AM to tell the Ponca story. On the next day, he met the prisoners in his own office to hear their story, a clear indication of his respect for Standing Bear and the Poncas.

Historic Edition of the Omaha Herald April 1, 1879

Tibbles walked back to his office at the *Omaha Herald* to transcribe his notes from the meeting at General Crook's office. He finished at 3:00 AM.[169] The *Omaha Herald* printed an historic edition of its newspaper on April 1, 1879. It was picked up by newspapers across the United States with favorable editorials in the *Chicago Tribune*, *Missouri Republican*, *New York Herald*, *New York Tribune*, and *New York Sun*. The article created a national interest in the Ponca tragedy.[170] The *Omaha Herald* reported the story in a series of headlines:

CRIMINAL CRUELTY

The History of the Ponca
Prisoners Now at the Barracks

A Tale of Cruelty
That was Never Surpassed

Now They Have Been
Wronged and Robbed

Gen. Crook Holds a Council with them.

The article contained detailed information of the Tibbles interview with the Ponca prisoners, transcribing the remarks of Buffalo Chip, Standing Bear, and Susette Primo, as well as a few words by Charles P. Morgan. Tibbles also reported the extraordinary meeting held at General Crook's office with Standing Bear and other Ponca chiefs. He concluded the article by providing the readers with a copy of the Omaha Clergy's Resolution to Carl Schurz.[171]

Newspaper Identifies the Prisoners

This same edition of the *Omaha Herald* listed the names of the twenty-six Ponca prisoners held at Fort Omaha:[172]

The Eight Men

Standing Bear (Ma-chu-nah-zha)
Buffalo Chip (Ta-zha-but)
Yellow Horse (Shan-gu-he-zhe)
Cries for War (Na-chen-ah-gaz)
Long Runner (Wa-the-ha-cuh-she)
Crazy Bear (Ma-chu-dun)
Little Duck (Me-tha-zhun-ga)
Buffalo Track (Ta-the-ga-da)

The Six Boys

Turtle Grease (Ka-wig-i-sha)
Walk in the Mud (Min-i-chuck)
Walk in the Wind (Ta-do-mon-e)
Coon's Tail (Me-gah-sin-de)
Big Mouth (E-tun-ka)
Swift (Wa-thi-ka)

The Twelve Women and Girls

Buffalo Cow (Ta-wau-oo)
Midst of the Sun (Me-he-da-wah)
Feather Crazy (Me-shud-da-de)
Yellow Spotted Buffalo (Za-zi-zi)
Walking Yellow (Za-on-a)
Grown Hair (No-zha-zhe)
Good Provision (Oo-moo-ah)
Wa-gang-wah
Little Buffalo Woman (Ta-nigh-ingah)
Susette Primo (Standing Bear's wife)
Midst of the Eagles (Me-he-da-wah)
Laura Primo (Susette's niece)

Note: Today, the name of Standing Bear is well known to many. However, few people know or have heard the names of his fellow prisoners, who were just as affected by the injustice, the physical and emotional sufferings, and the deaths of friends and family. Their homes, their land and their way of life were also taken from them.

Tibbles Seeks a Legal Solution

Thomas Tibbles had secured the support of the Omaha clergy and sent a telegram to President Hayes on their behalf. Tibbles had written a detailed report on the plight of the Poncas which his newspaper had published and disseminated nationally.

Yet, in spite of overwhelming support for the Poncas in various newspaper editorials in major cities, Secretary Schurz did not rescind his order.

General Crook would be forced to escort his prisoners back to Indian Territory as soon as the sick among them were able to travel. Time was running out.

Tibbles needed to find a lawyer.

Chapter 11

Legal Team Assembled

Tibbles faced a dilemma. A lawyer was needed to take on this unprecedented case. A lawyer was needed who had the creative skill to draft the pleadings and the persuasive skill to argue the case before a federal court judge for the first time in any American courtroom. Even if Tibbles could find such a lawyer, he would have to convince him of the historic importance of the case and the necessity of representing the prisoners for free.

Would any successful lawyer in Omaha be willing to risk his reputation and future standing in the community to represent this group of Native Americans? *Wolfe's City Directory* for 1878-1879 recorded that the population of Omaha was 26,215, including 59 active attorneys.[173] On the evening of April 2, 1879, Tibbles found his man.

John L. Webster

John Lee Webster was born on March 18, 1847 in Harrison County, Ohio. He was wounded in the Civil War. Thereafter, he attended Mount Union College in Ohio and Washington College in Pennsylvania. He settled in Omaha in 1869 by accident. He was headed to Wyoming to open a law office, but due to a blizzard, his train was forced to stay in Omaha for a week. During that time, he decided Omaha would be a good place to live and work. He became one of the most distinguished lawyers and civic leaders in the history of Omaha, serving in the state legislature, and for a few years as Omaha city attorney. Webster was President of the Nebraska Constitutional Convention in 1875. His law office was located at 244 Douglas Street in Omaha. At the time of the Standing Bear Trial, he was 32 years of age.[174]

Tibbles Calls on Webster

Tibbles had a connection with John Webster. Both had attended Mount Union College in Ohio. Tibbles went to Webster's home at 380 Chicago Street in Omaha to describe the facts of the case. Webster was moved, but said he needed to "take the matter under advisement." Tibbles returned in the morning and Webster agreed to take the case under one condition: Tibbles must secure the services of A.J. Poppleton as co-counsel.[175]

Andrew J. Poppleton

Andrew Jackson Poppleton was born on July 24, 1830 in Oakland County, Michigan. After the law firm he worked for in Detroit dissolved, he read an article in the New York Tribune about the new great city west of Council Bluffs. He set out to see it for himself. In his autobiography, *Reminiscences*, Poppleton wrote that while walking in downtown Omaha on October 14, 1854, he discovered that "there were perhaps twenty people on the site of the present city of Omaha, but there was no government, no courts, no laws. For legal work, it seemed an unpromising field." So, he decided to leave Omaha. While walking out of town, he ran into an old friend, A.J. Hanscom, from Michigan, who assured him a territorial organization was being set up and asked him to consider staying. Poppleton agreed and soon was elected to the first territorial legislature. He was the first lawyer to open a law office in Omaha in 1854. In fact, he built a 10' x 14' cottonwood/sod structure near 10th & Farnam Street that functioned as his home and law office. He served as Speaker of the Nebraska Legislature in 1857. In 1858, he was elected as Omaha's second mayor. Poppleton left private practice in 1863 to become general counsel for the Union Pacific Railroad. At the time of the Standing Bear trial, he was 49 years of age.[176] [177]

Tibbles Calls on Poppleton

On April 4, 1879, Tibbles met with A. J. Poppleton in his office located in the headquarters of the Union Pacific Railroad (the former Herdon House Hotel) located at the N.E. Corner of 9th and Farnam Street in downtown Omaha.[178] Poppleton listened carefully as Tibbles related the Poncas story. In his *Reminiscences*, Poppleton wrote why he agreed to take the case:

> I was requested to join Mr. J. L. Webster in an application for a habeas corpus to test the validity of the restraint of the liberty of Standing Bear for the purpose of removing him to Indian Territory. The question of whether the writ would lie on behalf of a tribal Indian and also whether the United States had any lawful power by its soldiery to remove him were wholly new and of vast importance. Without fee or reward or any hope or promise of compensation, Mr. Webster and myself entered upon this work and espoused the cause of the Indians.[179]

Standing Bear's Legal Team Assembled

Tibbles had done the job General Crook encouraged him to do. He brought together two of the most distinguished lawyers in Omaha to represent Standing Bear and the Ponca prisoners. Time was of the essence.

Now, it was up to the lawyers.

Andrew J. Poppleton
Attorney for Standing Bear & Ponca Prisoners
Omaha's First Practicing Lawyer
Courtesy from The Bostwick-Frohardt Collection owned by KM3TV and on permanent loan to The Durham Museum, Omaha, BF3217-077

John L. Webster
Attorney for Standing Bear & Ponca Prisoners
President of Nebraska Constitutional Convention (1875)
Courtesy of History Nebraska RG2141-23

Chapter 11 – Legal Team Assembled

Chapter 12

The Great Writ

The Latin term "Habeas Corpus" means "you have the body." When used in conjunction with a Writ it is called *"Habeas Corpus Ad Subjiciendum"* referring to a written judicial order directed to the person detaining another, commanding him to produce the body of the prisoner, or person detained before the court, to test the legality of the imprisonment or detention; not whether the person is guilty or innocent.[180]

Andrew J. Poppleton gave credit to General Crook for the idea of using a Writ of Habeas Corpus in this matter:

> It is within my personal knowledge that General Crook was the first person to suggest the remedy of habeas corpus. I believe him to have been the first person who ever conceived the idea that the great writ would lie at the suit of a tribal Indian. This, in my judgment, is not the least of his titles to the affection and gratitude of his country.[181]

After meeting with General Crook and writing his article for the *Omaha Herald*, Tibbles went to a law library in downtown Omaha to find a legal solution - some way to connect the Writ of Habeas Corpus to the Poncas. He had some familiarity with the law because he had worked in a law office in Winterset, Iowa, over twenty-five years earlier. After many hours of research, he found what he believed was the answer - the newly enacted 14th Amendment to the Constitution.[182]

The Fourteenth Amendment

The Fourteenth Amendment to the Constitution was enacted by Congress in 1866 and ratified by the states on July 28, 1868. Section 1. of the Amendment contained the key language:

> All persons born or naturalized in the United States, and subject to the jurisdiction thereof, are citizens of the Unites States and of the State wherein they reside. No state shall make or enforce any law which shall abridge the privileges or immunities of citizens of the United States; nor shall any State deprive any person of life, liberty, or property, without due process of law; nor deny to any person within its jurisdiction the equal protection of the laws.[183]

The Senate instructed the Judiciary Committee to "inquire into and report to the Senate the effect of the Fourteenth Amendment to the Constitution upon the Indian tribes of this country." Mr. Carpenter, chair of the committee, reported to the Senate on December 14,1870, saying:

> Volumes of treaties, acts of Congress almost without number, the solemn adjudications of the highest judicial tribunal of the republic, and the universal opinion of our statesmen and people, have united to exempt the Indian, being a member of a tribe recognized by, and having treaty relations with, the United States from the operation of our laws, and the jurisdiction of our courts. Whenever we have dealt with them, it has been in their collective capacity as a state, and not with their individual members, <u>except when such members were separated from the tribe to which they belonged</u>; and then we have asserted such jurisdiction as every nation exercises over the subjects of another independent sovereign nation entering its territory and violating its laws.[184]

Legal Strategy

Tibbles, Webster and Poppleton believed the only legal solution to stop General Crook from being forced to carry out the order to take the Poncas back to Indian Territory was to get Standing Bear and the other Ponca prisoners into federal court. To accomplish this task, the lawyers decided to file an Application for a Writ of Habeas Corpus before a federal court judge in order to place a hold on the government's order. This had never been done on behalf of Native Americans in any American court. Webster explained his thinking on the Writ to Tibbles:

> This is a question of vast importance. A Petition for such a Writ must be based upon broad constitutional grounds, and the principles involved in it underlie all personal liberty. It is a question of the natural rights of men, such as was discussed by the fathers and founders of this government. I am not satisfied that a Writ would hold on account of the peculiar relations of Indians to the government. They have always been treated as "wards," as incapable of making contracts, etc., but it will do no harm to try. It seems to me that there ought to be power somewhere to stop this inhuman cruelty, and if it does not reside in the courts where shall we find it? If Hon. A.J. Poppleton will assist me, I will go right to work and draw up the papers.[185]

Historical Background of the Writ

The first written expression of the Writ of Habeas Corpus occurred on June 15, 1215 when John, King of England, was forced to sign the *Magna Carta* at Runnymede, England. Today, 800 years later, the Magna Carta is considered one of the bulwarks of our freedom. Within its 63 clauses are two which speak to the purpose of the Writ:

> *Clause 39.* No free man shall be taken or imprisoned or disseized or outlawed or exiled or in any way ruined, nor will we go or send against him, except by the lawful judgment of his peers, or by the law of the land. *Clause 40.* To no one will we sell, to no one will we deny or delay right or justice.[186]

England formally adopted *The Habeas Corpus Act in 1679*, setting forth the process by which the Writ could be employed by a person accused of criminal behavior:

> That on complaint and request in writing, by or on behalf of any person committed and charged with any crime (except for treason or felony, expressed in the warrant, or as accessory, or on suspicion thereof), the Chancellor or a Judge shall award a Habeas Corpus for such prisoner, returnable immediately before himself or any other of the judges, and upon giving security to appear and answer to the accusation in the proper court of judicature....That the Writ shall be returned, and the prisoner brought up, within a limited time, according to the distances, not exceeding twenty days.[187]

In commentary on the 1679 Act, Sir William Blackstone, Justice in His Majesty's Court of Common Pleas, wrote in his *Commentaries on the Laws of England* (1750):

> The remedy, therefore, is now complete for removing the injury of unjust and illegal confinement. It frequently happens, that parties suffer a long imprisonment because they are forgotten.[188]

The Writ in American Law

Article I, Section 9. of the Constitution of the United States declared that "the privilege of the writ of habeas corpus shall not be suspended, unless when in cases of rebellion or invasion the public safety may require it."[189]

The First Congress enacted *The Judiciary Act of 1789* by which federal courts were granted power to hear applications for a writ of habeas corpus filed on behalf of persons jailed under federal authority.[190]

The Thirty-Ninth Congress enacted *The Habeas Corpus Act in 1867* by which the federal courts were granted an extended power to hear such applications for "any person restrained in violation of the Constitution, or of any treaty or law of the United States." [191]

President Lincoln Suspends the Writ

On April 27, 1861, President Abraham Lincoln told Winfield Scott, commanding general of the United States Army, that if there was armed resistance in Maryland against the federal troops traveling through the state on their way to defend Washington D.C. in the first month of the civil war, Scott or his officers in command were authorized to suspend habeas corpus in order to guarantee the safety of the troops.

One of Lincoln's concerns was that such armed resisters, without the suspension of habeas corpus, as Brian McGinty suggests, "could be freed almost overnight by pro-slavery judges," which would make it hard for the military to protect itself and its supply lines.[192]

Armed resistance came and bridges were destroyed. Members of the Maryland State Militia were arrested, including John Merryman, who was charged with treason against the federal government and taken to Fort McHenry for detainment. His lawyers filed an action in federal court and Chief Justice Roger B. Taney ruled that only Congress, not the President, had authority under the Constitution to suspend habeas corpus. However, Chief Justice Roger B. Taney did not order Lincoln to comply. So, Lincoln did not. Congress then passed the *Habeas Corpus Suspension Act* in 1863 authorizing the President to suspend habeas corpus during the remainder of the Civil War.[193]

The Poncas Application for a Writ April 4, 1879

IN THE DISTRICT COURT OF THE UNITED STATES, FOR THE DISTRICT OF NEBRASKA.

THE UNITED STATES EX REL. MA-CHU-NAH-ZHA (STANDING BEAR)

VS.

GEORGE CROOK, A BRIGADIER GENERAL OF THE ARMY OF THE UNITED STATES, AND COMMANDER OF THE DEPARTMENT OF THE PLATTE.

In the matter of the Application of Ma-Chu-Nah-Zha, Standing Bear et al. for a Writ of Habeas Corpus.

To the Honorable Elmer S. Dundy, Judge of the District Court of The United States for the District of Nebraska.[194]

The *Application for a Writ of Habeas Corpus* listed each of the names of the Ponca prisoners, and described the purpose of the Application:

> They, each, and all of them are prisoners unlawfully imprisoned, detained, confined and in custody, and are restrained of their liberty under and by color of the alleged authority of the United States by George Crook, a Brigadier General of the Army of the United States, and commanding the Department of the Platte, and are so imprisoned, detained, confined and in custody, and restrained of their liberty by said George Crook at Fort

> Omaha on a military reservation, under the sole and exclusive jurisdiction of the United States, and located within the territory of the District of Nebraska.[195]

After a brief description of the order under which General Crook held the Poncas in custody, the attorneys stated what would be the focal point of their argument:

> These complainants further represent that they are Indians, and of the nationality of the Ponca Tribe of Indians, but that for a considerable time before, and at the time of their arrest and imprisonment, as is herein more fully set forth, **they were separated from the Ponca Tribe of Indians, and had been and were separated from their tribal relations to said Ponca Tribe of Indians** and that so many of said Ponca Tribe of Indians as maintain their tribal relations are located in the Indian Territory.[196]

Poppleton and Webster described the Poncas at the time of their arrest and imprisonment:

> That your complainants at the time of their arrest and imprisonment were lawfully and peaceably residing on the Omaha reservation...by the consent of said Omaha Tribe of Indians...some of them were actually engaged in agriculture, and others were making preparations for immediate agricultural labors and were supporting themselves by their own labor, and no one of these complainants was receiving or asking support of the government of the United States. That your complainants were not violating and are not guilty of any violation of any law of the United States, civil or military, or of any treaty of the United States, for which said arrest and imprisonment were made.[197]

Poppleton and Webster concluded their Application for the Writ with the following plea:

> Wherefore, these complainants say that their said imprisonment and detention is wholly illegal, and they demand that a Writ of Habeas Corpus be granted directed to the said George H. Crook, a Brigadier General of the Army of the United States commanding the Department of the Platte commanding him to have the bodies of Ma-chu-nah-zha (Standing Bear) ... (*Note:* the names of the other prisoners are listed as well) ... before your honor at a time and place therein to be specified, to do and receive what shall, then and there be considered by your honor concerning them, together with the time and cause of their detention, and said Writ, and that the complainants may then be restored to liberty.[198]

Standing Bear and seven other Poncas signed the Application for the Writ, as did Poppleton and Webster as Attorneys for Petitioners. T.H. Tibbles and Lt. W.L. Carpenter signed as Witnesses. They all re-signed under oath before Homer Stull, a Notary Public on April 4, 1879.[199]

Where is the Judge?

The attorneys were now ready to file their Application in federal court and make their argument before the judge. However, Judge Dundy was out of town on a bear hunting trip. Tibbles reported that the judge's staff did not know where he was or when he would return.[200] Two days later, on Sunday evening, the judge returned home and sent a telegram notifying the attorneys that he would hear their application in his courtroom in Lincoln, Nebraska, in two days.[201]

Elmer S. Dundy

Elmer Scipio Dundy was born on March 5, 1830 in Trumbull County, Ohio. He was a teacher and principal of a school in Pennsylvania. At that time, he decided to study law and began his practice in 1853 in the County of Clearfield, Pennsylvania. Four years later, he settled in Falls City, Nebraska where he practiced law. He was elected to a four-year term in the Nebraska Territorial Legislature. President Andrew Johnson nominated him as the first Judge of the United States District Court for the District of Nebraska after Nebraska became a state in 1867. The Senate confirmed his appointment on April 9, 1868. He held this position for 28 years until his death in 1896. At the time of the Standing Bear trial, he was 49 years of age. [202]

April 8, 1879
Hearing on Poncas Application for Writ

Webster and Poppleton boarded the train in Omaha and traveled to Lincoln to appear before Judge Dundy in the federal district courtroom located in the State Capital Building on April 8, 1879. Watson B. Smith, Clerk of the federal court, endorsed the Application for the Writ. Judge Dundy issued the following ruling:

> It being made to appear to the Court that the said Petitioners are detained without any legal authority. It is therefore ordered, that a Writ of Habeas Corpus be allowed to issue on behalf of the said Petitioners directed to George Crook, a Brigadier General of the United States, commanding the Department of the Platte, returnable within ten days from the date of the service of said Writ upon him.[203]

Later that same day, General Crook was served the Writ by Ellis L. Bierbower, Deputy United States Marshall. Crook was now blocked from carrying out the order issued by Secretary Schurz to return the Poncas to Indian Territory. Nothing more could be done until a formal hearing could be convened in federal court. General Crook signed the *Return of Service* to confirm his receipt of the Writ on April 11, 1879, and it was filed in the court on April 18, 1879.

Response of the Government

On April 9, 1879, Carl Schurz directed the United States Attorney General to send a telegram to the Attorney General of the State of Nebraska stating:

> According to newspaper reports a writ of habeas corpus has been granted by Judge Dundy at Omaha in favor of Standing Bear a Ponca Indian and several others held as prisoners by the military. If such be the fact it is desirable to have the government represented in the case. I therefore request that the District Attorney at Omaha be instructed to inquire into the matter and to secure delay at the hearing of the writ until full information can be furnished by this Department. [204]

The period between the issuing of the Writ by Judge Dundy on April 8, 1879 and the opening of the Trial on May 1, 1879 was a time in which the government went public in its attempt to set forth its position that it had acted within its rightful authority to remove the Ponca tribe to Indian Territory. The government believed this small band of Poncas had left Indian Territory without government permission and should be ordered back. E. A. Hayt, Indian Commissioner to the Poncas, wrote a letter dated April 10, 1879 to Carl Schurz, Secretary of the Interior, in which he released to the press a summary of the government's position casting negative comments as to Standing Bear's character at the time of the move to Indian Territory:

> There is probably no finer location for an Indian settlement in the Indian Territory, and in all respects, it is far superior to their old location in Dakota, from which, in previous years, they had themselves asked the Department to remove them ... During my visit to the Agency I ascertained that Standing Bear was dissatisfied, but that he was the only one among the chiefs who showed a bad spirit, he was constantly grumbling ... If the reservation system is to be maintained, discontented and

> restless or mischievous Indians cannot be permitted to leave their reservation at will and go where they please.[205]

Standing Bear refuted Hayt's characterization by showing Tibbles a letter Hayt wrote on December 18, 1877, a few months after the tribe arrived in Indian Territory in which Hayt said:

> This is to certify that Standing Bear is a Chief of the Ponca Indians. This tribe is at peace with the United States, and Standing Bear is recognized as a chief of said tribe, whose influence has been to preserve peace and harmony between the Ponca Indians and the United States, and as such is entitled to the confidence of all persons whom he may meet.[206]

Standing Bear ended his remarks to Tibbles that day saying, "the commissioner did not give me a good character. I got my character by a long life devoted to the advancement of my tribe ... the commissioner may have intended no wrong to me in making the statement; but my voice has always been for peace."[207] [208]

Genio M. Lambertson

Genio Madison Lambertson was born on May 19, 1850 in Franklin, Indiana and died June 15, 1902 in Chicago, Illinois. He came to Lincoln, Nebraska in 1874 to practice law. In December 1878, he was appointed U.S. District Attorney for Nebraska, just five months before the Standing Bear trial and would serve in that post until 1887. He was active in the Lancaster County Bar Association. In later years, he served as an Assistant Secretary of the Treasury, and as attorney to the Interstate Commerce Commission. At the time of the Standing Bear Trial, he was 28 years of age.[209] Lambertson came from Lincoln to meet with General Crook in Omaha to go over the facts of the case with the General.

Genio M. Lambertson in his Law Office, 1900

Courtesy of Charles E. Wright of
Cline Williams Wright Johnson & Oldfather
Law Firm, Lincoln, Nebraska

Chapter 13

The Trial - Witnesses Testify

UNITED STATES ex rel. STANDING BEAR v. CROOK

(5 Dill.453, 25 F. Cas.695)
Circuit Court D. Nebraska. 1879.

This was a hearing upon return to writ of habeas corpus issued against George Crook, a brigadier general of the army of the United States at the relation of Standing Bear and other Indians, formerly belonging to the Ponca Tribe of Indians.

A.J Poppleton and John L. Webster, for relators.
G.M. Lambertson, U.S. Atty.
Dundy, District Judge.

Date and Place: May 1, 1879, Omaha, Nebraska

The trial began on Thursday morning, May 1, 1879, in the Federal Courthouse in Omaha, Nebraska. It concluded late in the evening of May 2, 1879. The start date of May 1st was confirmed by Lieutenant John Bourke who sat next to General Crook at the trial,[210] and by Thomas Tibbles who reported in the May 2, 1879 edition of the *Omaha Herald*, "the Ponca Indian habeas corpus case was begun yesterday morning."[211]

Note. The term "Relator" was used in the trial proceedings to identify the person (Standing Bear and the other Ponca prisoners) upon whose complaint or at whose instance the Writ of Habeas Corpus was issued.

Office of the Federal Court, Omaha, NE, 1879
Courtesy from The Bostwick-Frohardt Collection owned by KM3TV and on permanent loan to The Durham Museum, Omaha, BF828-003-5

The federal court was located at 15th & Dodge in a three-story building, known as the U.S. Customs House.[212] The U.S. Post Office was located on the first floor. The Railway Mail Service and the U.S. Court administrative offices occupied the second floor. The U.S. Customs Office shared the third floor with the federal courtroom and jury room. No American court had ever witnessed what was about to take place in that third-floor room.

Attendees

Men and women of all ranks of society in Omaha, including members of the clergy, local lawyers, and newspaper reporters, were in attendance in the courtroom to witness the trial. Omaha had four daily newspapers at the time of the trial: *Omaha Herald*, *Omaha Bee*, *Omaha Republican*, and *Omaha Evening News*.[213] These local newspapers were crucial to bringing this historic civil rights case to the attention of the national press, and hence to the general public.[214] [215]

Of all the newspapers in Omaha at the time of the trial, the *Omaha Herald* had gained a national reputation among newspapers on the east coast, due in large part to the aggressive approach taken by its founder George L. Miller to promote Omaha as "the future chief city of the Missouri Valley." Miller had founded the newspaper in 1865, when he was just thirty-five years of age. Miller came from New York to Omaha in 1854, the same year as Andrew Poppleton. By the time he opened the newspaper's doors, he had a variety of occupations, including "doctor, territorial politician, real estate speculator, businessman, and post sutler at Fort Kearney."[216]

For a city of slightly over 26,000 residents, Omaha was a bustling and diverse community. It boasted three banks, four concert halls, four colleges, twelve schools, thirty-two hotels, thirty-six physicians, four railroads, two hospitals, four bowling alleys, twenty-seven billiard halls, eighteen barbers, one cooper, three gunsmiths, five livery stables, four ice dealers, two steamboat agents, three undertakers, four breweries, thirteen fire stations, and seven dentists (including the author's great uncle John Dwyer located at 695 16th Street), three telegraph companies, one streetcar railway, and four singing societies. There were 26 Christian church denominations: three Baptist, four Catholic, two Congregational, three Episcopal, five Lutheran, six Methodist, two Presbyterian and one Unitarian; and one Jewish synagogue.[217]

The major reporter of the trial was Thomas H. Tibbles, deputy editor of the *Omaha Herald.* He sat directly behind the Relators table where he observed and recorded all that occurred over the next two days. He made it his personal crusade to publicize the plight of the Poncas.

General George Crook, in full dress uniform, sat at the table alongside his legal counsel, District Attorney Genio M. Lambertson. Sitting behind the General was his aide-de-camp, Lieutenant John G. Bourke, along with Colonel Horace B. Burnham, Judge Advocate for the Military Department of the Platte.[218]

Standing Bear walked into the courtroom in his full chief regalia. He was escorted by Lieutenant William L. Carpenter and took his place near his legal counsel, John L. Webster and Andrew J. Poppleton. With Standing Bear was his wife Susette Primo and a grandson, the child of his deceased daughter Prairie Flower. Yellow Horse and Buffalo Chip were also in the courtroom.[219]

The Court provided Standing Bear with an interpreter since he understood little English. However, the interpreter, William Hamilton, was there only to interact between the judge, attorneys and Standing Bear when questions were posed to him. There is no evidence that Hamilton said anything else to Standing Bear during the trial.

Standing Bear and the other members of his tribe with him understood nothing of what was going on in the courtroom. The presence of Native Americans in a federal courtroom was new – there was no precedent. Standing Bear likely felt uncomfortable knowing his fate and that of his family and friends was in the hands of strangers.

Near Standing Bear was Bright Eyes, his cousin of the Omaha Tribe. She spoke both English and the Ponca language fluently and would serve as a trusted interpreter for him if he would be granted the opportunity to speak on his own behalf. Her father, Iron Eye, Chief of the Omaha Tribe, sat next to her.

Court Convened

At 10:00 AM, Judge Elmer S. Dundy entered the courtroom and gaveled the court into session. Attorneys for both sides identified themselves and their clients. Judge Dundy presented a statement of the facts of the case before the Court and directed the lawyers to proceed.

Procedural Matters Discussed

At first "the lawyers were somewhat puzzled as to the mode of procedure to be followed in the case, and various questions were discussed. There was some talk between the attorneys and court about the pleadings, and what the issue in the case really was."[220]

Poppleton said it was "the duty of the United States to establish the jurisdiction of the military to hold the Indians;" and the hearing should proceed upon the sufficiency of the *Return of the Writ*, whether it shows valid ground for the deprivation of the liberty of the Indians." Lambertson replied that Poppleton should have filed a demurrer or made a motion to quash, for "unless something of that kind was done, he didn't see how an issue could be raised" regarding the validity of the arrest and imprisonment of the Poncas.[221]

Lambertson expressed his frustration that he had received a letter from the United States Department of the Interior concerning the issue of whether the Poncas had dissolved their tribal relations, but he could not offer it into evidence because it had not been sworn.[222]

The letter Lambertson referred to was dated April 22, 1879 signed by E.J. Brooks, Acting Commissioner for the Department of the Interior. The letter begins with Brooks saying to Lambertson:

> I am in receipt of your communication of the 14th instant, in relation to the Application by certain Ponca Indians for a Writ of Habeas Corpus, and in which you ask for a statement of the various treaties made with the Ponca Indians; the causes which led to their removal to the Indian Territory; the reason for their deserting their reservation, etc.[223]

In his letter, Commissioner Brooks provides some details of the various treaties signed by the Poncas, and then acknowledged that the 1868 Fort Laramie Treaty took land from the Poncas and gave it to the Sioux "without the consent of the latter Indians." Brooks then gave his justification for the Ponca removal, saying:

> As the Poncas and Sioux had been bitter enemies for many years, it became necessary to remove the Poncas from their reservation to save them from the destruction that would be likely to overtake them from the location of the Sioux on the Missouri River.[224]

The final part of Brooks letter to Lambertson demonstrated his callous assessment of the condition of the Ponca tribe in Indian Territory:

> During the first few months of their residence in the Indian Territory, they lost a large number by death, which is inevitable in all cases of removal of Northern Indians to a Southern latitude.[225]

In spite of not having this letter available to offer into evidence, Lambertson informed the court "he was willing to proceed and consider the question of whether they had dissolved their tribal relations."[226]

The attorneys discussed other procedural matters and then the Judge directed Webster to call his first witness.[227]

Relators' First Witness - William W. Hamilton

Webster called William W. Hamilton to the stand. After being sworn under oath, Hamilton testified he had worked as a clerk in the Agency store on the Omaha reservation for six years, having lived among the Omaha tribe for over 12 years. He spoke the same language as the Omaha and Ponca Indians. He stated that his father had been a missionary to Native American tribes, including the Omahas, for over 30 years.[228]

Webster asked Hamilton to identify the wife and grandson of Standing Bear in the courtroom and to describe the condition of Standing Bear's family when they arrived at the village of the Omaha tribe on March 4, 1877. Hamilton had seen them there at that time.[229]

Webster's strategy in calling Hamilton to the stand was to elicit testimony that would prove to the court that these Ponca prisoners intended to forever sever their tribal relations when they left Indian Territory. He would do so in three lines of questions posed to this witness.

The first line of questioning concerned the clothing worn by the Poncas when they arrived at the Omaha Tribe village, March 4, 1879. Webster wanted to show that the Poncas did not dress in the typical clothes expected of Native Americans living in a tribal environment, but they dressed as any white persons would dress:

Webster: How were they supplied as to clothing?

Hamilton: They had blankets, some of them, and some had coats; those that had coats wore pants and were dressed in citizens' clothes.[230]

Next, Webster wanted to prove that the prisoners were not a group from a tribe with no personal identity, but lived in separate family units, married with children, the same as any white family:

Webster: You may state whether or not they were divided into families at the time when they came – whether they were married and composed families as man and wife?

Hamilton: They were.

Webster: And the children were children of these families?

Hamilton: Yes sir, some of them were orphans, living with their relations.

Webster: Which ones do you speak of as being orphans?

Hamilton: There were two orphans came with them. There is one (indicating a young Indian boy who was present with the Relators in the courtroom) sitting in the woman's lap. The other is at camp.

Webster: Whose son is this one here?

Hamilton: He is the grandson of Standing Bear.

Webster: Who is this woman who sits here?

Hamilton: She is the wife of Standing Bear.

Webster: What is her name?

Hamilton: Susette.[231]

Webster's third line of questioning to this witness showed the court that the intent of the Ponca prisoners was to be self-supporting farmers, not dependent upon the government:

Webster: State what these Indians were engaged in after they arrived at the Omaha Agency?

Hamilton: What little time they stayed there they were engaged in helping the Omahas put in their crops.

Webster: State what ones, if any, of the Indians, the Poncas, were putting in crops for themselves?

Hamilton: Buffalo Chip was helping put in a crop for himself. His friends at the Omaha Agency gave him land enough to sow his wheat.

Webster: At the time of the arrest, state, if you know, about the amount of wheat Buffalo Chip had put in on this land which was set apart for him?

Hamilton: I think there must have been four or five acres sowed.

Webster: State how many of these Poncas during their stay at the Omaha Agency, were engaged in labor- whether all were so engaged?

Hamilton: All that were able to, were.

Webster: Those who were not employed in actual labor, state why they were not?

Lambertson: Objection. Immaterial.

Judge: Overruled.

Webster: You may answer.

Hamilton: Because they were sick and unable to work. [232]

Lambertson rose to cross-examine Hamilton in an attempt to get him to describe Standing Bear as a chief of the Ponca tribe and to acknowledge that the Poncas had brought government property with them from Indian Territory, including wagons, clothes and tents, and had received supplies from the agency store which employed this witness. Lambertson was successful in getting Hamilton to agree that not all of the Poncas went to farming ground given to them by the Omaha tribe. He wanted to demonstrate to the court that Webster's contention was incorrect.[233]

Lambertson asked Hamilton a series of questions to show the Court that the prisoners were not self-supporting individuals as Webster had contended, but instead were dependent on aid from the government:

Lambertson: What did they live in – tents?

Hamilton: Yes sir, they brought their tents, I think.

Lambertson: These tents were provided by the government?

Hamilton: These tents were made by themselves.

Lambertson: These wagons were furnished by the government.

Hamilton: Yes sir; they brought their wagons with them.

Lambertson: Did they have any citizens' clothes?

Hamilton: Yes sir; some were, and some were not.

Lambertson: Some of them wore blankets?

Hamilton: Some wore blankets, pants and vests, and some wore Indian clothes throughout.

Lambertson: These blankets were supplied by the government?

Hamilton: Some of them – yes sir.[234]

In Webster's re-direct examination, followed by Lambertson's re-cross examination, both sides questioned Hamilton as to whether the Poncas were under the control of the Omaha tribe while living on their reservation; in effect, exchanging life on one reservation for another.

Lambertson: Is there any head man in the Omaha Tribe?

Hamilton: No sir, not now. There was some time ago, last summer, but they put away all their chiefs and head men.

Webster: They live like white men, then?

Hamilton: They try to. [235]

Relators' Second Witness – Lieut. Carpenter

Hamilton left the witness stand and returned to his seat near Standing Bear. Webster then called his second witness, Lieutenant William L. Carpenter. After being sworn on oath, Webster asked Lieutenant Carpenter to confirm that he had been the arresting officer of the Poncas on March 27, 1879, and to describe the Poncas' physical condition when he transported them to Fort Omaha. Carpenter replied that the Poncas were "dressed in citizen's clothes" and some "were willing to work; they had been sick for some time."[236]

On cross-examination, District Attorney Lambertson asked Carpenter what appeared to be a simple question, but one that resulted in the following exchange between the two lawyers and Judge Dundy:

Lambertson:	How many chiefs are there?
Webster:	Objection, question is improper cross-examination.
Judge:	Sustained.
Lamberton:	State the names of the parties arrested.
Webster:	Objection, question is immaterial, and the returns show that.
Judge:	Why is that material?
Lambertson:	To show these Indians have their chiefs, to whom they profess allegiance.
Judge:	You will have to make the witness your own to do that.[237]

Court adjourned for lunch.

Relators' Third Witness - Standing Bear

Court reconvened at 2:00 PM.[238] Judge Dundy directed Webster to call his next witness. Webster called Standing Bear to the stand. Standing Bear and his court-appointed interpreter, William H. Hamilton, were sworn under oath. District Attorney Lambertson immediately objected to Standing Bear being called as a witness.[239] Lambertson was doing his duty as prosecuting attorney to seize this issue at the first opportunity. He correctly reasoned that the United States Supreme Court had already determined that Native Americans were "wards of the Government," not persons; therefore, Standing Bear had no right to testify in an American courtroom.[240]

Judge Dundy overruled his objection saying, "(A)nybody can be sworn. This court recognizes no distinction on account of race, color, or previous condition."[241] The Judge had already committed himself to give Standing Bear and the other Relators their day in court when he granted their *Application for a Writ of Habeas Corpus* on April 8, 1879, so he likely wasn't ready to stop the proceedings this early in the trial.

Note: A witness is "one who, being present, personally sees or perceives a thing; a beholder, spectator, or eyewitness. One who testifies to what he has seen, heard, or otherwise observed."[242]

Webster's questions to Standing Bear, through his Interpreter William Hamilton, were brief. The witness's answers were equally brief. The dialogue between attorney and witness focused on what Standing Bear's family life was like when living in the Dakota/Nebraska region, in contrast to what life was like for him and the Poncas in Indian Territory.[243]

Then, Webster asked Standing Bear to tell the story of how he and his people lived in Indian Territory. Lambertson objected to this question saying the hearing was "solely as to whether these Poncas have dissolved their tribal relations." But before the judge could rule on his objection, Lambertson withdrew it. Webster told the interpreter to proceed with his question. Standing Bear then spoke at length, as interpreted by William H. Hamilton:

> When we got down there, we saw that the land was not good; kick off the soil and you found stones and it was not fit to farm. They promised us money and clothing, but we have seen very little of it yet. We could not do anything; we had no strength in our bodies at all, and we kept getting weaker every day. The tribe was dying off. 158 died, I think. God wants me to live. What have I done that I am brought here! I do not know. It seems as though I have no place on earth. I want a place where I can work and support my family, and when done with life, die peaceably.[244]

At this point, Standing Bear raised his voice while testifying to such a volume that Judge Dundy instructed him "not to get excited, but to take things coolly."[245]

Webster began another series of brief questions to which Standing Bear replied with equally brief answers:

Webster: How many were in the tribe when you left the Territory?

S. Bear About 581.

Webster: How many came away with you when you came up?

S. Bear Thirty.

Webster: Why did you come up to the Omaha agency?

S. Bear I thought I might save my wife and one child I have left.

Webster: How many of your own children died in Indian Territory?

S. Bear Two died down there. My son could talk English; could read and write and was a great help to me with the white people. It makes me feel very bad when I think of it.[246]

Then, Webster posed a question to Standing Bear in an attempt to establish that Standing Bear's intent in leaving Indian Territory was to live the remainder of his life in his homeland and not return to the Ponca tribe in Indian Territory. Webster wanted to prove an intent to disassociate themselves from their tribe. Standing Bear said, "if I ever came back it would not be to stay."[247]

Finally, Webster asked Standing Bear about his role as a chief:

Webster: After you left the tribe in Indian Territory did you exercise your authority as a chief over those who came with you?

S. Bear I didn't consider myself a chief. I looked upon myself as on a level with the rest.[248]

In his cross-examination of Standing Bear, Lambertson asked him the number of people in his band of which he was chief ("about fifty"); how many of that band had followed him up north ("about thirty"); and had he taken any government-supplied wagons and mowing machines during his journey north ("two of the wagons they have were given to them on their former reservation, and the other is one he bought himself").[249]

Lambertson concluded his cross-examination of Standing Bear with two key questions:

Lambertson:	Were you chief or head man over these Indians in Indian Territory?
S. Bear:	I don't count myself as a chief.
Lambertson:	When you left did you inform the agent that you were going to take care of yourself?
S. Bear:	I told the agent I wanted to go back. We would all die there and that I was going away to save the lives of my family and make a living. I wanted to go on to my own land, land that I had never sold. There is where I wanted to go. My son asked me when he was dying to take him back and bury him there, and I have his bones in a box with me now. **I want to live there the rest of my life and to be buried there.** [250]

Webster informed the judge he had no more witnesses to call.

No Government Witnesses

Judge Dundy directed Lambertson to call his first witness. But Lambertson did not call any.[251]

Note. Before the trial began, Lambertson may have believed that because the law considered an Indian to be a "ward of the government" and not a "person," the Judge would grant a motion to dismiss the case and quash the Writ for lack of standing. So, he likely believed there was no need to prepare any person to testify on behalf of the government. When he objected to Webster calling Standing Bear to testify and was quickly overruled by Judge Dundy, he likely realized his mistake. On the other hand, who could he have called as a witness? Calling General Crook to testify may have backfired due to Crook's known respect for Native Americans.

Closing Arguments - Postponed

Judge Dundy turned to Webster and Poppleton and instructed them to begin their closing argument. They had expected Lambertson to call some witnesses of his own, so they were not fully prepared to make their closing arguments that late in the day. But Judge Dundy insisted he continue. So, Webster stood up and started to speak. Tibbles reported in the *Omaha Herald* what happened next:

> There were many ladies, citizens and army officers present and the atmosphere was stifling. Mr. Webster had uttered but a few sentences when he informed the judge that it was impossible for him to proceed, and sat down, apparently very ill. [252]

Court adjourned until 10 o'clock the next morning.[253]

Postscript

Tibbles followed Standing Bear and the other prisoners back to Fort Omaha. He wanted to talk with him about the day's proceedings. Standing Bear wanted to speak to him as well. Standing Bear informed Tibbles of his frustration with the happenings in the courtroom that day. He didn't feel he was allowed to speak for himself. He asked Tibbles to relate his wishes to the judge so he could plead his own cause, in his own words. Tibbles returned to his office to write a summary of the activities of the first day of the trial for the *Omaha Herald* newspaper[254]

Chapter 14

The Trial - Closing Arguments

Thomas Tibbles said that before court resumed, he met in private with Judge Dundy and related to him Standing Bear's request to speak to the court. Judge Dundy consented.[255]

The line of questioning during the first day of the trial focused on whether Standing Bear and the other Ponca prisoners had severed their ties to the Ponca tribe, with the intent to live on their own, as individuals, outside of Indian Territory.

As the lawyers honed their closing arguments, they did so with full knowledge that they needed to convince only one man, Elmer S. Dundy. The Judge alone would decide the outcome of this case. This was a bench trial, there was no jury.

A Case of "Firsts"

This was a case of "firsts".

For the first time in the history of American jurisprudence, a lawyer stood in a federal courtroom representing a client who was a Native American. A client who was not a person in the eyes of the law. A client who was not a citizen in the eyes of the law. It had never been done before.

For the first time in the history of American jurisprudence, a judge was hearing a cause of action previously reserved for white people only.

This was a case of "first impression," meaning it had no precedent for lawyers or for judges. It had never been done before.

Challenges Facing the Lawyers

Webster and Poppleton were faced with an unprecedented challenge. They must be creative as well as factual in their closing arguments to persuade the judge of his legal authority to rule favorably on behalf of their clients. The first hurdle was to convince the judge their clients were human beings and that the Writ should be confirmed.

Lambertson began the trial believing the judge had legal authority to dismiss the case since the law considered Native Americans to be "wards of the government" not "persons."[256] Therefore, because the Relators were not persons under the law, they had no standing or right to appear in court and the Writ should be quashed.

As Lambertson prepared for the second day of the trial, he likely had some doubt in his mind because this judge had demonstrated his willingness to listen to the Relators' witnesses. When Lambertson questioned Standing Bear's right to testify, Judge Dundy likely surprised him with the reply, "anybody can be sworn, this court recognizes no distinction on account of race, color or previous condition."[257] As the second day of the trial was about to begin, Lambertson likely realized this was not an open-and-shut case.

Court Convened - May 2, 1879

On Friday May 2, 1879, the second day of the trial began. Judge Dundy entered the courtroom at 10:00 AM. Tibbles reported that "as on the day previous there was a large number of ladies and leading citizens present all deeply interested in behalf of the Poncas."[258]

Timeline – Day 2

Based upon the accounts of the trial given in the *Omaha Herald*, Webster spoke for approximately three hours, Lambertson spoke for approximately three hours, Poppleton spoke for just over two hours, and Standing Bear spoke for nearly thirty minutes. The following is an approximate timeline of the second day of the trial:

10:00 AM	Court convened. Webster speaks for two hours.[259]
12:00 PM	Court recessed.[260]
1:30 PM	Court re-convened. Webster speaks "about an hour more."[261]
2:30 PM	Lambertson speaks "for nearly three hours."[262]
5:30 PM	Court recessed.[263]
7:30 PM	Court re-convened. Poppleton speaks "for over two hours."[264]
9:30 PM	Poppleton concludes.[265]
10:00 PM	Standing Bear closed his speech at "nearly 10 o'clock"[266]

Closing Argument of John L. Webster

The May 3, 1879, edition of The *Omaha Herald* reported that Webster spoke for two hours, stopping at 12 o'clock when court recessed. At 1:30 PM court reconvened, and Webster spoke for about an hour more.[267]

During his three-hour discourse, Webster attempted to convince the judge that the Writ should be confirmed, and the Relators released from the hands of the government. To do so, he laid out a series of arguments beginning with a matter-of-fact statement that the Omaha tribe had "the right to invite their friends (i.e, Standing Bear and his companions) to dwell with them and share the land...for their title is good, they have the use and occupancy in which they cannot be disturbed."[268] Webster believed there was no legal authority to prevent Standing Bear from staying with his cousins the Omaha tribe, or going back on his own land in the Niobrara River valley.

He based this argument believing the rights of Native Americans were "acknowledged when this continent was first discovered. They are based upon great principles which never change. They are like the law of nations. The government cannot change them." [269]

Webster quoted a letter written in 1805 to an Indian Chief by Thomas Jefferson in which the President declared, "these lands can never go from you, but when you wish to sell." Webster concurred saying the government cannot take their lands "from them by treaty or otherwise, without their free consent."[270]

Building upon this argument, Webster attacked what he considered to be a misinterpretation of the "doctrine of discovery":

> The principle accepted by all European nations who had made discoveries on this continent, was that it gave them no absolute authority over the inhabitants who occupied the discovered countries or ownership of the soil against the original occupants, but it gave them a title good against other European claimants. That was all there was in a title by discovery! Did the landing of a few whites upon the shores of the Atlantic give them a title to the lands which the Poncas then owned and occupied. No such claim as this has ever been made. Discovery only gave a title to lands which were unoccupied. [271]

In his next argument, Webster stated that he believed Indian tribes had been considered by the government as independent nations, saying that the government "acknowledged their national character in making treaties with them. They had their own government and their own laws ... these Omaha and Poncas are not savages nor wanderers. They cultivate the soil, live in houses, and support themselves."[272]

Tibbles reported that Webster quoted "many authoritative sources that Indian Tribes maintaining their organization as such were separate and independent nations and had all the rights and privileges of such except what they had relinquished by special treaty stipulations."[273]

Webster said it naturally followed from this line of thinking:

> If these Indians belonged to the Ponca tribe and their tribal relations were unbroken that they had a right as an independent nation to go back to their land which they still owned, or the Omaha tribe had a right to receive them into their nation, and there was no power in the government of the United States to interfere.[274]

Webster provided Judge Dundy authority upon which he could base his ruling - the newly passed Fourteenth Amendment to the United States Constitution. He quoted Section 1. thereof:

> All persons born or naturalized in the United States, and subject to the jurisdiction thereof are citizens of the United States and of the state wherein they reside. No state shall make or enforce any law which shall abridge the privileges or immunities of citizens of the United States; nor shall any state deprive any person of life, liberty or property, without due process of law; nor deny to any person within its jurisdiction the equal protection of the laws.[275]

Webster told the court that when an Indian severed his tribal relations, he stopped his allegiance to his tribal chiefs and thereby became a citizen of the United States. He quoted from a Report made by the Senate Judiciary Committee in 1870:

> It is pertinent to say, in concluding this report, that treaty relations can properly exist with Indian tribes or nations only, and that, when the members of a tribe are scattered, they are merged in the mass of our people, and become equally subject to the jurisdiction of the United States.[276]

Webster briefly discussed the plight of Standing Bear and the Ponca people and the great deprivations and sufferings they had endured in being taken against their will by the military, with no justifiable reason under the law. The Poncas had committed no crime against the government or any white settlers. By frequently referring to the Poncas as "prisoners of war" and at the same time calling them "persons" and "citizens," Webster intended to emphasize to the court the injustice of their arrest and imprisonment. He concluded his remarks with a passionate plea for freedom:

> They have fled with their wives and children from this pestilential prison, and now ask the protection of the court. They say we are men; we have a right to go where we please. We are citizens of the United States. In the words of Frederick Douglas, a man belongs to himself. His hands are his own, his feet are his own, his body is his own, and they will remain his until you storm the citadel of heaven, and wrest from the bosom of God, man's title deed to himself.[277]

Webster sat down. He had given a passionate argument backed by authoritative sources. He had done his job in laying the foundation for his clients to be freed. Tibbles reported that Webster's words were "especially brilliant and powerful and made a deep impression on all present."[278]

Closing Argument of Genio M. Lambertson

United States District Attorney Lambertson found himself sandwiched between two experienced and eloquent lawyers who quoted not only from legal sources, but also from the writings of ancient philosophers, to make their arguments. Despite the fact a jury would not decide this case, Lambertson was likely aware that opposing counsel was holding before the court the recently adopted Fourteenth Amendment. This was something the judge could rely upon as authority in deciding the case. As Webster concluded his remarks, Judge Dundy directed Lambertson to make his closing argument.

At approximately 2:30 PM Lambertson rose to speak. Tibbles reported that he "spoke for nearly three hours." He began with an unusual tribute to the "generosity" of opposing counsel "coming to the assistance of these poor people, prisoners and friendless in a strange land."[279]

The *Omaha Herald* did not give as much coverage to Lambertson's closing argument, especially in light of the coverage given to the arguments made by Webster and Poppleton. However, the May 3, 1879, edition of the newspaper provided its readers with a concise summary of the major points Lambertson made to the Court saying that a Native American:

1) Has no standing to come into the court;
2) Is not entitled to a writ of habeas corpus;
3) Is not a citizen;
4) Indian tribes are not independent, but dependent communities;
5) Judge Taney's ruling in the Dred Scott decision should be binding on this case. [280]

Lambertson entered into a lengthy discussion of the Writ of Habeas Corpus, and then posed two questions to the court: "has the court, or judge sitting at chambers, jurisdiction of this case?" and "if the court has jurisdiction, is such a case presented as to warrant the court in discharging the petitioners?"[281] Lambertson did not believe that the court had any power to adjudicate this matter saying:

> To come within the jurisdiction of the court, the complainants' must be either a foreign subject or a citizen of one of the states, or the case must arise under the laws of the United States, the constitution or treaties. The complainants were not citizens or subjects of a foreign state, and they were not citizens of the United States. The

> Fourteenth Amendment did not apply to them, for the complainants had not dissolved their tribal relations.[282]

The major focus of Lambertson's closing argument can be confirmed by Judge Dundy in his ruling when he remarked "the District Attorney discussed at length the reasons which led to the origin of the writ of habeas corpus, and the character of the proceedings and practices in connection therewith in the parent country."[283]

It can be inferred from Judge Dundy's language in his decision that Lambertson also spent considerable time defending the government's decision to arrest the Relators for leaving Indian Territory without government permission; noting that Lambertson denied that "the Relators had withdrawn and severed, for all time, their connection with the tribe to which they belonged."[284]

It appears Lambertson had done an admirable job in presenting his case to the Court:

Judge Dundy:	The district attorney has supported his theory with an argument of great ingenuity and much ability.[285]
Thomas Tibbles:	These positions he defended with a great deal of shrewdness and power, and in every way performed the duties of his office with credit to himself. [286]

It was after 5:30 PM when the District Attorney took his seat. Judge Dundy had allocated only two days for the trial because he had other business waiting for him in Lincoln. He adjourned the proceeding for supper.[287]

Closing Argument of Andrew J. Poppleton

After the court re-convened for an unusual evening session, the Judge directed Andrew J. Poppleton to deliver his closing argument. Towards the end of his life, Poppleton recalled how that moment impacted him:

> Without fee or reward or any hope or promise of compensation, Mr. Webster and myself entered upon this work and espoused the cause of the Indians. The hearing took place before District Court Judge Dundy at Omaha. I delivered my argument upon that case in the evening in the large court room of the Federal Building on the corner of Dodge and Fifteenth Streets. There were present in addition to the court and its officers, an audience taxing the fine capacity of the room, including General Crook and other officers under his command, and many ladies. I have spoken to larger audiences, but I think never to one more intelligent and sympathetic, and in looking back I cannot now recall any two hours work of my life with which I feel better satisfied. [288]

The *Omaha Herald* allocated the largest number of columns for the closing argument of Andrew Poppleton, practically more than Webster and Lambertson combined. The May 4th, 1879 headline read:

A PLEA FOR THE PONCAS

The Argument of Hon A.J. Poppleton
to the Habeas Corpus Case

What the Great Writ of Liberty
Really Means

It Applies to Every Human Being
on the Face of the Earth
How the Power of Forty Millions
of People is used to Crush a
Few Helpless Indians

A Powerful Appeal for the Down
Trodden, who for Two Hundred
Years Have had None
to Defend Them

Interesting Scenes and Incidents
in the Court Room

Tibbles began his report on Poppleton's closing argument by saying the audience in the courtroom "listened with breathless attention to every word.... From the very start it was a masterly speech, but the latter portion was intensely thrilling and powerful."[289]

Poppleton began his closing argument by saying:

> May it please the Court. I suppose it would be impossible for counsel under any circumstances to approach a case of this character without a feeling of oppression at its magnitude and the consequences involved in it....It is intensified in this case by the fact that I am to appear here on behalf of a feeble remnant of a class of beings who

> seem, for two or three hundred years to have had no friends and to have never had any rights.[290]

Poppleton immediately questioned Lambertson's argument against the Relators' Application for a Writ of Habeas Corpus by saying:

> I confess I have been somewhat surprised as to the character of the argument made here. What is it in effect, is that these relators have no right whatever, not even the right of petition, not even the right to the protection of their liberty. What is the reason in that?[291]

Poppleton asked why the government didn't offer concrete evidence of a particular law giving them the right to remove the Poncas to Indian Territory. He also asked why the government did not disclose any Treaty broken by the Poncas to justify its actions. After all, Poppleton said, the burden of proof was on the government:

> If there is any contract, any agreement of any description whatever which justifies the government in trying to hold these people in the Indian Territory, that contract lies in its possession, and had something like a month to prepare for this hearing and it should have produced it here, to show to the Court some premise and some reason why the Indians are sought to be held.[292]

He stayed in this line of argument for a few minutes, as he wondered aloud how the District Attorney could make the assertion that the Poncas were without any rights by saying:

> Our government has gone and made treaties with them in which the government has undertaken to guarantee them certain rights, certain lands and certain privileges in connection with these lands, and now to turn back on those guarantees is a most infamous act, because it is treachery on the part of power as against weakness.[293]

Poppleton discussed the erroneous Dred Scott decision and gratefully acknowledged that it had been rectified by the Fourteenth Amendment. He noted, however, that during that struggle, the writ of habeas corpus was employed successfully on behalf of fugitive slaves. At the same time, Poppleton expressed his "feeling of humiliation when the great government of the United States comes here with no better argument than that these Indians have no rights whatsoever."[294]

Then Poppleton told the court he believed Lambertson's suggestion that the Indians lost all their rights via the Indian Appropriation Act of 1871 was wrong, saying: "Your Honor may not have noticed one of the significant provisions of that Act which said clearly that 'it should not be construed as abrogating any treaty theretofore entered into with any Indian Tribe." Poppleton pointed to a specific clause in the 1858 Ponca Treaty which said a certain tract of land near the Niobrara River is "reserved for the future home of said Indians" and the government agreed to "protect these Indians in possession of this tract of land reserved for their future home, and their persons and property thereon."[295]

In Poppleton's point of view, Lambertson erred when he told the Court that the government had "given" the Poncas tools, houses and plows, when, in effect, this was not a gift but "consideration" for the relinquishment of their rights to certain land they were ceding to the government. It was a contractual arrangement, Poppleton argued, that did not authorize the government to unilaterally change the terms of the treaty when the Poncas had not broken its end of the bargain.[296]

Poppleton spent a considerable portion of his time analyzing the 1858 and 1865 Ponca Treaties and promises made to the tribe. He also discussed the terrible injustice done to the Poncas by the government's 1868 Fort Laramie Treaty with the Sioux by saying:

> One thing the government undertook to do, at any rate, was to give away the rights of the Poncas north of the

> Niobrara to the Sioux. Will any man stand here and contend there is any good faith in that, any honor in that? Is there any justice in that?[297]

Poppleton's reputation as a passionate trial lawyer was displayed often in his two hours before the court as these words demonstrate:

> I tell your Honor it is an outrage – and the word outrage doesn't express it – it is an infamy difficult to grasp.... Is it possible that this great government, standing here dealing with this feeble remnant of a once powerful nation, claims the right to place them in a condition which is to them worse that slaves, without a syllable of law; without a syllable or contract or treaty? I don't believe, if your Honor please, that the courts will allow this; that they will agree to the proposition that these people are wild beasts; that they have no status in the courts. The argument of the gentleman representing the government comes to that - they are simply wild beasts.[298]

That led Poppleton into a discussion on "this great Writ that for five hundred years has been the shield and protection of individual liberty until it has made every man a sovereign the world over." He strongly believed that the prisoners had the right to petition the court for a writ of habeas corpus to:

> Protect themselves against lawless violence because everything in this county not done by law is lawless violence. In looking over judicial decisions I found this language: '*No human being in this country can exercise any kind of public authority which is not conferred by law. In the United States it must be given by the express words of a written statute. Whatever is not given is withheld and the exercise of it is positively prohibited.*' If there is any power in the military to hold these people, it must be under a positive statute. I protest against the power of the military to arrest them, and I think the military itself has a right to protest.[299]

Just as Poppleton was returning to a brief discussion of the use of the Writ for the benefit of a fugitive slave, a dramatic moment occurred in the Courtroom. District Attorney Lambertson abruptly interrupted Poppleton's speech with a question:

> Lambertson: After the Dred Scott decision, did a slave ever invoke the Writ in a Federal Court?
>
> Poppleton: No. After that there probably was no opportunity to invoke it. It was repeatedly invoked before ... In this country now, Judge Taney's decision has gone out of date, and I don't see how it is possible to bring the Indians under any disability under the Fourteenth Amendment, unless some express laws can be produced to that effect.[300]

Lambertson sat down. Toward the end of his argument, Poppleton restated something Standing Bear had said in court that deeply affected him:

> During the sixty days I was coming from the Indian Territory to the Omaha agency I carried the bones of my boy in a box, and I have got them now. It is my sacred desire, it is my absorbing purpose, it is my highest aspiration to carry the ashes of that boy and bury them where in his last hours he wished to be buried. [301]

Poppleton paused and looked at Standing Bear. Then he said:

> That man not a human being?
> Who of us all would have done it?

> Look around this city and state and find, if you can, the man who has gathered up the ashes of his dead son, wandered for sixty days through a strange country without guide or compass, aided by the sun and stars only, that the bones of his son may be buried in the land of their birth.
>
> No! It is a libel upon religion; it is libel upon missionaries who sacrifice so much and risk their lives in order to take to these Indians that gospel which Christ proclaimed to all the wide earth, to say that these are not human beings. But if they are human beings they cannot be barred from the right to this Writ.[302]

Poppleton was finished. It was nearly 9:30 PM.[303]
Court adjourned.

But Judge Dundy did not rise and leave the courtroom.
He remained on the bench.

The evening was not over.

Chapter 14 - The Trial – Closing Arguments

Chapter 15

Standing Bear's Historic Speech

At approximately 9:30 PM on May 2, 1879, the three attorneys had finished their closing arguments. They had spoken, collectively, for over eight hours. Court was adjourned. For all intents and purposes, the trial was over. Everyone was waiting for the U.S. Marshall to call them to rise as the judge left the courtroom. But Judge Dundy did not leave.

Instead, the Judge motioned Standing Bear to speak.[304] Bright Eyes stood ready to interpret his words to those gathered in the courtroom at that late hour.

Bright Eyes

Susette LaFlesche (*Inshata-Theamba*) of the Omaha Tribe was known as 'Bright Eyes.' She was born in Bellevue, Nebraska, in 1854, the daughter of Iron Eye (Joseph LaFlesche) Chief of the Omaha tribe, and Mary Gale LaFlesche. Her grandfather, John Gale, was a surgeon in the U.S. Army. Bright Eyes learned to read and write English while attending the Presbyterian Mission Boarding Day School located on her tribal land near Decatur, Nebraska. For a number of years, she attended the prestigious Elizabeth Institute for Young Ladies in New Jersey. Upon graduation, she became a teacher in the Omaha Agency School. She and her father listened intently to the horrible story their cousin Standing Bear told them when he and his companions arrived in their village on March 4, 1879. Standing Bear would have felt very comfortable with Bright Eyes interpreting his words for the judge because she was fully knowledgeable of his story and fluent in both the Ponca and English languages.[305]

Standing Bear's Desire to Speak

When he had been called to the witness stand on the first day of the trial, Standing Bear became frustrated as the lawyers on both sides asked him leading questions and interrupted his answers.

As grateful as he was for the effort his lawyers expended on his behalf, Standing Bear wanted an opportunity to speak. In that way, he believed the judge could hear all of the facts regarding the injustice, sufferings and deaths his people had endured. He wanted the judge to know what the government had done to his people. He wanted to tell his own story. [306]

Note: Judge Dundy had no legal precedent to guide him in deciding whether to grant Standing Bear's request. There is no written evidence as to whether Judge Dundy gave prior notice to the three lawyers of his decision to allow Standing Bear to speak at the end of the trial. However, one can assume he did give prior notice, because there is no evidence that any of the attorneys raised an objection.

The moment had arrived.
A special opportunity was being afforded to a special man.

The Historic Moment

Tibbles reported that after Poppleton sat down, "Judge Dundy said that Standing Bear had made a request to address the court. He supposed that to grant such a request would be entirely unprecedented, but he should grant the request. He supposed that it was the first time in the history of the country that an Indian ever addressed a court."[307]

Rising from where he had been sitting, Standing Bear turned sideways, half-facing the audience and half-facing the judge. He held his red blanket with his left hand. Then, after a brief moment, he turned to face the judge and "stretched his right hand out before him, holding it still so long that the audience grew tense."[308]

Everyone in the courtroom must have had their eyes fixed on him wondering if maybe the moment was too emotional for him, or maybe he was tired due to the lateness of evening and the close air in the room.

Standing Bear's words were interpreted by his cousin, Bright Eyes, and preserved for history by Thomas Tibbles. "At last, looking up at the judge," Standing Bear began:

> I see a great many of you here.
> I think a great many are my friends.
> Where do you think I came from?
> From the water? From the woods?
>
> God made me, just as he made all of you, and
> God put me on my land.
>
> But a man I did not know came and
> ordered me to leave my land.
> I objected.
> I looked around for a friend to help me,
> but there was none.
>
> Now I have found someone (casting his eyes towards
> his attorneys) and it makes me glad. [309]

Standing Bear then told the story of the Poncas forced move to Indian Territory and the death of 158 of his people. He said he did not want to die there. He came away to save his wife, his children, his friends. He wanted to go home, to bury the bones of his dead son, and to live out the remainder of his life in the land of his fathers. He never tried to hurt a white man. He then related that once, when out hunting, he found an American soldier on the prairie, almost frozen. He took him home, made him warm, and fed him until he could go away.[310]

Then, Standing Bear raised his hand to the perpendicular and held it there saying:

> That hand is not the color of yours.
> But if I pierce it, I shall feel pain.
> If you pierce your hand, you also feel pain.
> The blood that will flow from mine, will be
> the same color as yours.
> **I AM A MAN.**
> The same God made us both.[311]

The courtroom was silent. Everyone listened intently as Standing Bear paused ... then, turning towards an open window in the courtroom and looking up into the evening sky, Standing Bear spoke in a metaphor:

> I seem to stand on the bank of a river.
> My wife and little girl are beside me.
> In front the river is wide and impassable, and behind are perpendicular cliffs.
> No man of my race ever stood there before.
> There is no tradition to guide me.
>
> A flood has begun to rise around us.
> I look despairingly at the great cliffs.
> I see a steep, stony way leading upward.
> I grasp the hand of my child and my wife follows.
> I lead the way up the sharp rocks, while the waters rise behind us.
>
> Finally, I see a rift in the rocks, and
> I feel the prairie breeze strike my cheek.
> I turn to my wife and child with a shout that we are saved. We will return to the Swift Running Water that pours down between the green islands.
> There are the graves of my fathers.
> There again we will pitch our tipi and build our fires.
>
> **But a man bars the passage**!

> He is a thousand times more powerful than I.
> Behind him, I see soldiers as numerous as leaves on trees.
> They will obey that man's orders.
> I too must obey his orders.
> If he says that I cannot pass, I cannot.
> The long struggle will have been in vain.
> My wife and child and I must return and sink beneath the flood. We are weak and faint and sick. I cannot fight.

Then looking directly at Judge Dundy, Standing Bear said:

> **You are that man!** [312]

Reaction in the Courtroom

Standing Bear sat down. Tibbles described the dramatic scene:

> It was nearly 10 o'clock when Standing Bear closed his speech which was greeted with a round of applause. [313]
>
> I saw tears on Judge Dundy's face. General Crook sat leaning forward, covering his eyes with his hand. There was absolute silence for a moment, then the whole room rose at once with a great shout. Among the first to reach Standing Bear was General Crook. The entire audience came crowding after him to shake the chief's hand.[314]

The local and national reporters hurried outside to chronicle the story for their readers.

The lawyers, clergy, civic leaders, and general public walked down the three flights of stairs and out into the streets of downtown Omaha, tired, hot and likely emotionally drained. They had just witnessed history being made.

The soldiers loaded Standing Bear and the other Poncas onto wagons for the four-mile trip back to Fort Omaha. They entered the courtroom as prisoners; they left as prisoners. Whether they would ever be free again was out of their control.

One man would decide that question. They would have to wait ten days for his decision.

Note: Standing Bear's eloquent words in his various recorded speeches cannot be called into question as being invented by an interpreter or a reporter since three different interpreters (Charles Morgan, William Hamilton and Bright Eyes) and two different reporters (Thomas Tibbles and Lieutenant John G. Bourke) at different times in 1879 (March 30, March 31, May 1, and May 2) and at different locations (Fort Omaha, General Crook's office and the Federal Courthouse) demonstrate.

- ◊ Charles Morgan interpreted Standing Bear's remarks, as reported by Thomas Tibbles on March 30, 1879 on the grounds of Fort Omaha *(Chapter 10).*
- ◊ Charles Morgan again interpreted Standing Bear's remarks as reported by Lieutenant John Bourke on March 31, 1879 in General Crook's office *(Chapter 10).*
- ◊ William Hamilton interpreted Standing Bear's testimony during the trial on May 1, 1879 as reported by Tibbles *(Chapter 13).*
- ◊ Bright Eyes interpreted Standing Bear's historic speech on May 2, 1879 as reported by Thomas Tibbles *(Chapter 15).*

All three interpreters and both reporters reflect the same poetic beauty and spirit of Standing Bear. The metaphor can be found in its entirety in Tibbles autobiography *Buckskin and Blanket Days.*

Note: The metaphor is similar in tone and imagery to Standing Bear's speech made in General Crook's office at Fort Omaha on March 31, 1879 as recorded by Lieutenant John G. Bourke.[315] Tibbles may have decided not to include the metaphor in his May 4, 1879 newspaper report in order to protect the reputation of Judge Dundy from the public who were not in the courtroom that day to see and hear Standing Bear point to the judge saying, "You are that man." The judge said in his ruling that he was acutely aware that he would be criticized either way. So, Tibbles may have felt recording what Standing Bear said about the judge could create a public outcry of disrespect to the court. This could have made it more difficult for the judge to rule in favor of the prisoners. The account of the speech in the *Omaha Republican* newspaper for May 4, 1879 is similar in many respects to the account given in the *Omaha Herald* on the same date. However, the ending in the *Omaha Republican* does not contain the closing metaphor.

Finally, Standing Bear's eloquence was confirmed by Caroline L. Poppleton, wife of attorney Andrew J. Poppleton, when she wrote in 1915, the words he spoke in her home on May 20, 1879:

> Out of the wealth of his human soul, and out of the fullness of his manly heart, he uttered sentiments, and expressed purposes among ten thousand.[316]

Chapter 16

A Time for Waiting

For the next ten days, everyone involved in the case waited for Judge Elmer S. Dundy to render his decision.

Standing Bear and his companions waited on the grounds of Fort Omaha, prisoners of General George Crook. They wondered what the future held for them:

- ◊ Would they ever be allowed to go home?
- ◊ Would they ever be allowed to live their lives and raise their children as they desired?
- ◊ Would they be forced to go back to a land they found hopeless, full of death?

Standing Bear and his wife must also have wondered whether they would be allowed to bury the bones of their beloved son, Bear Shield. They loved him and wanted above all else to be able to fulfill his dying wish – to be buried in the soil of his ancestors so as to walk in the afterlife in the comfort of his people, not alone.

Tibbles went back to work at his desk in the offices of the *Omaha Herald* writing the happenings of the trial for his readers in Omaha that would be picked up by other newspapers throughout the nation. Tibbles wrote a record of these two historic days. He transcribed his detailed notes made while sitting behind the Relators table. He described the timing of what happened in the courtroom, the substance of the questioning of witnesses, the objections raised by the lawyers, the comments of the judge to the objections raised, and the closing arguments made by the three lawyers. He also gave us a record of Standing Bear's speech. Tibbles was the scribe of history.

Judge Dundy spent the week pondering the facts of the case and the arguments he had heard. He researched statutes, treaties, and the historic relationship the Poncas had with the government. The Judge was aware he would be criticized whichever way he ruled, saying:

> As the matter furnishes so much valuable material for discussion, and so much food for reflection, I shall try to present it as viewed from my own standpoint, without reference to consequences or criticisms, which, though not specially invited, will be sure to follow. [317]

If he ruled in favor of the Relators, Judge Dundy would likely be criticized by white settlers who wanted the land cleared of Native Americans to move onto it themselves, and by the government/military who wanted to preserve the reservation system in Indian Territory. At the same time, if he ruled in favor of the government, an outcry of injustice would likely be directed at him from the media, clergy and supporters of Native American reform.

Three Distinguished Lawyers

Webster, Poppleton and Lambertson went about their business as usual. Each lawyer in his own way likely wondered if he should have called another witness, asked another question, raised another objection, included just one more point in his closing argument, or maybe even wished he would have been better off if he had left something unsaid. It is not unusual for lawyers to rehash a case after it is over; sometimes even second-guessing themselves. But at some point, every trial lawyer has to let the matter rest knowing he or she did the best they could, at the time, and under the circumstances. Hindsight never won a case.

In 1832, the year George Catlin came to the Ponca village to study their culture and paint their portraits, a French political scientist, Alexis deTocquiville, spent nine months on the East coast observing the workings of the American democracy and questioning how this young democracy was working. The conclusion he reached is of interest because of the crucial role lawyers played in the United States at that time. deTocquiville wrote:

> In visiting the Americans and studying their laws, we perceive that the authority they have entrusted to members of the legal profession, and the influence which these individuals exercise in the government, is the most powerful existing security against the excesses of democracy.[318]

Webster, Poppleton and Lambertson were admirable in their representation of their clients in unprecedented circumstances. They were forced to be creative in questioning and cross-examining witnesses, in making objections, and most especially in delivering their closing arguments. They had no case law to rely upon as precedent to support their positions.

These three distinguished Nebraska lawyers stood before the Court in a place no other lawyer had ever stood in the history of American jurisprudence. No other lawyer anywhere in the United States, not in Boston, St. Louis, New York, Chicago, or any other city, had ever stood in a federal courtroom to argue such a case. Never.

Lambertson had no choice but to participate in this case. He was assigned to represent the government. It was his duty as the District Attorney. If he deserves any criticism, it would fall on his failure to realize the potential ramification the Fourteenth Amendment to the Constitution could have on the case.

Webster and Poppleton on the other hand, did have a choice. They could have said "no" to Thomas Tibbles. They could have told him he was asking something no experienced lawyer would want to spend time on, especially when they were asked to do it for free. After all, there were fifty-seven other lawyers in Omaha at the time. They could have simply told Tibbles to find someone else. Instead, they agreed to take the case while understanding the challenge presented to them, as Poppleton later wrote:

> The question of whether the writ would lie on behalf of a tribal Indian and also whether the United States had any lawful power by its soldiery to remove him were wholly new and of vast importance. Without fee or reward or any hope or promise of compensation, Mr. Webster and myself entered upon this work and espoused the cause of the Indians.[319]

Standing Bear's Effect

Aside from the unknown effect the Fourteenth Amendment would have on the outcome of this case, there was something else at play in the courtroom –someone else – Standing Bear!

None of the three lawyers, or the judge, or any other person sitting in the Courtroom those two days in May 1879, were prepared for the effect this man would have on them as they listened to him speak and observed his bearing, dignity, eloquence, and passion. Standing Bear had a nobility about himself, a commanding presence, similar to Ponca Chief Shoo-de-ga-cha whom George Catlin had come to know and paint while visiting the Ponca Tribe in 1832.

No one captured the attention of those in the audience more than Standing Bear. His very presence towered above everyone else in the courtroom. He could not be ignored. His cause could not be dismissed. A decision must be made.

On May 12, 1879, the lawyers and reporters gathered in the courtroom anxiously awaiting the decision. Standing Bear was present to hear his fate and that of his companions.

Standing Bear knew he was a person, a human being, made by God. He did not need a judge to tell him that.

But he knew that his people and all Native Americans needed the judge to say it.

Justice cried out for it to be said.

The time had come for it to be said.

America needed to hear it.

Chapter 16 - A Time for Waiting

Chapter 17

The Court's Decision

The headline on the front page of the May 13, 1879 edition of the *Omaha Herald* captured the essence of Judge Elmer S. Dundy's historic decision rendered the previous day.[320]

STANDING BEAR VICTORY

Judge Dundy Issues an Order
Releasing the Ponca Indians.

A Decision Far Reaching In Its Effects

There is no Law for Using the Military
To Force Indians from one
Place to Another

The Indian Ring is Shorn of its Power

An Indian has Some Rights Which
The Courts will Protect

United States ex rel. Standing Bear v. George Crook 5 Dill.453, 25 F. Cas. 695 was reported in the Circuit Court Reports for Cases determined in the United States Circuit Courts for the Eighth Circuit, officially certified by John F. Dillon.[321]

Opening Remarks of Judge Dundy

Judge Dundy began his opening remarks by saying:

> During the fifteen years in which I have been engaged in administering the laws of my country, I have never been called upon to hear or decide a case that appealed so strongly to my sympathy as the one now under consideration.[322]

He then contrasted the two parties represented in the courtroom:

> On the one side, we have a few remnants of a once numerous and powerful, but now weak, insignificant, unlettered and generally despised race; on the other, we have the representatives of one of the most powerful, most enlightened, and most Christianized nations of modern times... We have the representatives of this wasted race coming into this national tribunal of ours, asking for justice and liberty to enable them to adopt our boasted civilization, and to pursue the arts of peace...and...we have this magnificent, if not magnanimous government resisting this application with the determination of sending these people back to the country which is to them less desirable than perpetual imprisonment in their own native land.[323]

Note: Judge Dundy mirrored some of Poppleton's passionate words spoken at the conclusion of his closing argument:

Andrew Poppleton	Judge Dundy
"earliest possessors of this soil"	"once numerous and powerful race"
"through a strange country"	"a country...less desirable"
"land of their birth"	"their own native land"
"gospel of Christ"	"Christianized nations"
"human beings"	"people"

Following a compliment "to the heart and mind of the brave and distinguished officer who is made respondent herein" (General George Crook), Judge Dundy concluded his opening remarks by acknowledging his responsibility in making this landmark decision:

> In a country where liberty is regulated by law, something more satisfactory and enduring than mere sympathy must furnish and constitute the rule and basis of judicial action. It follows that this case must be examined and decided on principles of law, and that unless the Relators are entitled to their discharge under the constitution or laws of the United States, or some treaty made pursuant thereto, they must be remanded to the custody of the officer who caused their arrest, to be returned to Indian Territory, which they left without the consent of the government.[324]

Confirmation of the Process

Judge Dundy described how this matter came before the court. He listed the date when the Relators made Application for a Writ of Habeas Corpus, the date he issued the Writ, the date service was made upon General Crook and its return. He declared all steps in the process had been properly executed.

Issue Number One - Jurisdiction

Judge Dundy proceeded to discuss the first issue before the court: jurisdiction. The District Attorney raised the question of whether this court had jurisdiction to issue the Writ on behalf of these Relators, much less hold a hearing regarding the matter.

After referencing Lambertson's initial concern, Judge Dundy immediately said, "I am of the opinion that his premises are erroneous, and his conclusions, therefore, wrong and unjust. He did not think "it necessary to examine the English laws regulating the suing out of the writ," saying instead that "this only proves that the laws of a limited monarchy are sometimes less wise and humane that the laws of our own republic."[325]

Citing Sections 751-753 of the Revised Statutes, Judge Dundy said, "when a person is in custody or deprived of his liberty under color of authority of the United States, or in violation of the constitution or laws or treaties of the United States, the Federal Judges have jurisdiction, and the Writ can properly issue."[326]

Are the Relators therefore entitled to the Writ, the judge queried? Answering his own question in light of these statutes, the judge said, "They certainly are, because they are in custody of a federal officer under color of authority of the United States; and because they are restrained of liberty in violation of a provision of their treaty."[327] Judge Dundy earlier referenced the Treaty of 1858 in which the government guaranteed the Poncas a certain tract of land near the Niobrara River for their permanent home.

Addressing the requirement in the Habeas Corpus Act of 1867 that an applicant must be "persons" or "parties" to be entitled to the Writ, Judge Dundy said:

> It nowhere describes them as *citizens*, nor is citizenship in any way or place made a qualification for suing out the Writ, and in the absence of express provision or necessary implication which would require the interpretation contended for by the District Attorney, I should not feel justified in giving the words *person* and *party* such a narrow construction.[328]

Judge Dundy employed a common principle in interpretation of specific words saying that "the most natural, and therefore most reasonable way is to attach the same meaning to *words and phrases* when found in a statute that is attached to them when and where found in general use." Quoting attorney Webster in his description of a person "as a living soul; a self-conscious being; a moral agent; especially a living human being; a man, woman or child; an individual of the human race," Judge Dundy agreed that "this is comprehensive enough, it would seem, to include even an Indian." He then made a precedent-setting statement:

> **I must hold, then, that *Indians,* and consequently the Relators, are *persons,* such as are described by and included within the laws before quoted.**[329]

The second element of the issue the District Attorney had raised was whether a federal court was the proper forum to hear the Relators' *Application for a Writ*, since it had never been heard in any federal court. "This is a *non sequitur.*" Judge Dundy concluded "I confess I do not know of another instance where this has been done, but I can also say that the occasion for it perhaps has never before been so great."[330]

Note: The Latin term "non-sequitur" means "it does not follow." That is to say – the inference does not follow from the argument.[331]

Complementing the Relators for seeking a peaceful redress of their grievances in this tribunal rather than resorting to armed resistance, Judge Dundy said that this tribunal "is the only one into which they can lawfully go for deliverance;" and it is irrelevant that "none of their ancestors ever sought relief thereunder."[332]

Judge Dundy concluded his remarks on this first issue, saying:

> It would indeed be a sad commentary on the justice and impartiality of our laws to hold that Indians, though natives of our own country, cannot test the validity of an alleged illegal imprisonment in this matter, as well as a subject of a foreign government who may happen to be sojourning this county.[333]

Issue Number Two - Expatriation

Ruling that the Relators qualified as "persons" to make an Application for a Writ of Habeas Corpus, and that this federal court was the proper forum to hear it, Judge Dundy moved on to what he considered to be "a question of much greater importance...which when determined, will be decisive of this whole controversy...the right of the government to arrest and hold the Relators for a time, for the purpose of being returned to a point in the Indian Territory from which it is alleged the Indians escaped."[334]

In deciding this second issue, Judge Dundy stated that he reviewed the government policies employed with the Ponca Tribe, including the Treaties of 1858 and 1865. He recognized the fact that the Poncas "have been at peace with the government, and have remained the steadfast friends of the whites, for many years; they lived peaceably upon the land and in the country, they claimed and called their own."[335] He cited the government's Treaty of 1868 with the Lakota Sioux in which their guaranteed land was taken from them "without consultation with, or knowledge or consent on the part of, the Ponca tribe of Indians."[336]

Judge Dundy recalled the testimony of Standing Bear in which he described the effects the move to Indian Territory had on his people, including severe illness and death. It was the reason he gave for his decision "to leave Indian Territory and return to his own home." Then, something quite remarkable happened. Judge Dundy inserted in his decision an actual quote that Standing Bear made on the witness stand that all he wanted "was to live and die in peace and be buried with his fathers."[337]

Judge Dundy proceeded to summarize the time, place and intent of the Relators at the moment the military arrested them on March 25, 1879. He described Standing Bear's testimony that he and his companions left the reservation in Indian Territory with the intent to sever their ties to their tribe forever, and to bury the bones of his dead son in his native land. Judge Dundy concluded that "such instances of parental affection, and such love of home and native land, may be heathen in origin, but it seems to me that they are not unlike Christian in principle."[338]

Then Judge Dundy continued saying, "this being so, it presents the question as to whether an Indian can withdraw from his tribe, sever his tribal relation therewith, and terminate his allegiance thereto, for the purpose of making an independent living and adopting our own civilization?"[339]

He concluded with this finding:

> I think the individual Indian possesses the clear and God-given right to withdraw from his tribe and forever live away from it as though it had no further existence. If the right of expatriation was open to doubt in this country down to the year 1868, certainly since that time no sort of question as to the right can now exist.[340]

Quoting Section 1999 of the Revised Statutes as proof of the meaning of the Fourteenth Amendment on this issue, Judge Dundy said:

> Whereas the right of expatriation is a natural and inherent right of all people, indispensable to the enjoyment of the rights of life, liberty and the pursuit of happiness ... Therefore, any declaration, instruction, opinion, order or decision of any officer of the United States which denies, restricts, impairs, or questions the right of expatriation, is declared inconsistent with the fundamental principles of the republic.[341]

In the last portion of his decision, Judge Dundy said, "I have searched in vain for the semblance of any authority justifying the Commissioner in attempting to remove by force any Indians to any place or any other purpose than what has been stated."[342]

Judge Dundy was not going to deny the authority of the government in these matters, but he was going to weigh its actions against the strict confines of the applicable statutes. He stated that the Ponca Indians were not at war with the government, were not violating any treaty their tribe had entered into and were not disturbing the peace and welfare of the Omaha tribe. Therefore, if they wanted to separate themselves from their tribe, the government "could not lawfully force them back to Indian Territory, to remain and die in that county, against their will...I must conclude that no such arbitrary authority exists."[343]

Ruling

Judge Elmer S. Dundy rendered his landmark ruling, saying "the reasoning advanced in support of my views, leads me to conclude:

1st. That an *Indian* is a PERSON within the meaning of the laws of the United States, and has, therefore, the right to sue out a writ of *habeas corpus* in a federal court, or before a federal judge, in all cases where he may be confined or in custody under color of authority of the United States, or where he is restrained of liberty in violation of the constitution or laws of the United States.

2nd. That General George Crook, the respondent, being commander of the military department of the Platte, has the custody of the relators, under color of authority of the United States, and in violation of the laws thereof.

3rd. That no rightful authority exists for removing by force any of the relators to the Indian Territory, as the respondent has been directed to do.

4th. That the Indians possess the inherent right of expatriation, as well as the more fortunate white race, and have the inalienable right to "*life, liberty,* and the pursuit of happiness," so long as they obey the laws and do not trespass on forbidden ground. And,

5th. Being restrained of liberty under color of authority of the United States, and in violation of the laws thereof, the relators must be discharged from custody, and it is so ordered.[344][345]

ORDERED ACCORDINGLY.

Judge Elmer S. Dundy
Courtesy of History Nebraska RG2411-1421-1

STANDING BEARS VICTORY.

Judge Dundy Issues an Order Releasing the Ponca Indians.

A Decision Far Reaching in its Effects.

There is no Law for Using the Military to Force Indians from one Place to Another.

The Indian Ring is Shorn of its Power.

An Indian has Some Rights Which the Courts will Protect.

SYLLABUS.

United States ex rel. Standing Bear vs. George Crook, a Brigadier General of the Army of the U. S. Before Elmer S. Dundy, U. S. District Judge for Nebraska. Habeas Corpus.

An Indian is a *person* within the meaning of the habeas corpus act, and as such is entitled to sue out a writ of Habeas corpus in the federal courts, when it is shown that the petitioner is deprived of liberty under color of authority of the United States, or is in custody of an officer in violation of the constitution, or a law of the United States, or in violation of a treaty made in pursuance thereof.

The right of expatriation is a natural, inherent, and inalienable right, and extends to the Indian as well as to the more fortunate white race.

The commissioner of Indian affairs has ample authority for removing from an Indian reservation all persons found thereon without authority of law, or whose presence may be detrimental to the peace and welfare of the Indians.

The military power of the government may be employed to effect such removal. But where the removal is effected, it is the duty of the troops to convey the persons so removed by the most convenient and safe route, to the civil authorities of the judicial district in which the offence may be committed, to be proceeded against in due course of law.

In time of peace no authority, civil or military, exist for transporting Indians from one section of the country to another without the consent of the Indians, nor to confine them to any particular reservation against their will, and where officers of the government attempt to do this, and arrest and hold Indians who are at peace with the government for the purpose of removing them to, and confining them on, a reservation in the Indian Territory, they will be released on habeas corpus.

A. J. Poppleton
and
Jno. L. Webster,
For the Relators.
G. M. Lambertson
U. S. Attorney for the Government.

The Omaha Herald, May 13, 1879

Chapter 18

Justice Awakened

When he heard Judge Dundy's ruling, Standing Bear was in the courtroom with his lawyers and Bright Eyes, his faithful interpreter. With a sense of relief that he and his companions were now free and would not be forced back to Indian Territory, Standing Bear realized he needed to find a place to live and an opportunity to bury his son.[346]

Response of the Government

The May 15, 1879, edition of the Omaha Herald reprinted a story from Washington D.C. concerning a statement by E.A. Hayt, Commissioner for Indian Affairs, made the previous day:

> The decision of Judge Dundy at Omaha in the Standing Bear habeas corpus case in which he virtually declares Indians citizens with the right to go where they please, regardless of treaty stipulations is regarded by the government as a heavy blow to the present Indian system, that if sustained will prove extremely dangerous alike to whites and Indians. If the power of the government to hold Indians upon their reservations and to return them when they escape is denied, the Indians will become a body of tramps moving without restraint wherever they please and exposed to attacks of frontiersmen without redress from the government. The district attorney at Omaha has been instructed to take the necessary steps to carry the question to higher courts.[347]

Webster and Poppleton gave a report to the Omaha Ponca Indian Committee on July 13, 1880, in which they explained what happened:

> The U.S. District Attorney took the case to the United States Circuit Court for this District by appeal, and about May 19th, upon hearing before Mr. Justice Miller, Associate Justice of the Supreme Court of the United States, was there continued, and on January 5th, 1880, the appeal was dismissed on the motion of the U.S. District Attorney.[348 349]

Why did "the U.S. District Attorney dismiss the appeal?" Journalist Helen Hunt Jackson wrote a letter on January 9, 1880, to Interior Secretary Carl Schurz asking him a series of questions on various matters concerning the desire of the Ponca tribe to sue the government to recover their lands taken from them by the "clerical error" in the Treaty of Fort Laramie in 1868. Schurz replied to her letter on January 17, 1880, and addressed the dismissal of the appeal:

> As I understand the matter, money is being collected for the purpose of engaging counsel to appear for the Poncas in the courts of the United States, partly to represent them in the case of an appeal from Judge Dundy's habeas corpus decision, and partly to procure a decision for the recovery of their old reservation on the Missouri River. I believe that the collection of money for these purposes is useless. An appeal from Judge Dundy's habeas corpus decision can proceed only from the Government, not from the Poncas, for the simple reason that the decision was in favor of the latter. An appeal was, indeed, entered by the United States District-Attorney at Omaha immediately after the decision had been announced. Some time ago his brief was submitted to me. On examining it, I concluded at once to advise the attorney-general of my opinion that it should be dropped, as I could not approve the principles upon which the argument was based. The attorney-general consented to

instruct the district–attorney accordingly, and thus Judge Dundy's decision stands without further question on the part of the Government. Had an appeal been prosecuted and had Judge Dundy's decision been sustained by the court above, the general principles involved in it would simply have been affirmed without any other practical effect than that already obtained. This matter is therefore ended. [350]

Response of the Indian Bureau

In the same May 15, 1879 edition of the *Omaha Herald*, Tibbles reacted strongly to telegrams he had received concerning the response of the Indian Bureau in Washington to fight the decision:

> The Indian Bureau has taken sudden alarm at the decision of Judge Dundy. The *Chicago Times* slops and sloshes around at the opinion without pretending to even state what the opinion is, or the principle upon which it was made. The telegrams inform us this morning that the idea prevails in Washington that Judge Dundy has knocked the infamies called the Indian policy of highway robbery into everlasting smithereens and takes about the same idiotic view of Judge Dundy's decision that the *Chicago Times* has done. Let the Washington herd of lawless reprobates hold their peace for a while. They forget that the very purpose for which the holy writ of habeas corpus was invoked for the protection of Standing Bear and his people was not to violate but to vindicate the laws, and the rights of an oppressed people under the laws....The wrongs of Government upon these Ponca Indians are lawless wrongs. They are monstrous wrongs. They cry to Heaven for redress from the lips of millions of good men and women all over our land, and a growing public opinion demands justice for a helpless and defenseless people.[351]

Standing Bear Attempts to Bury His Son

Standing Bear and his Ponca companions would face arrest if they stepped foot on any other tribe's reservation, including their ancestral land now held by the Lakota Sioux. So, Webster and Poppleton warned him not to go onto any reservation land. Evidently, a representative of the government contradicted his lawyers and told him it was alright to go onto his old homeland.[352]

Standing Bear may have been afraid or confused by these two contradictory statements; we do not know. But, sometime during the evening hours of May 13, 1879, Standing Bear slipped out of Fort Omaha by himself to go back to his old homeland to bury the bones of his son. General Crook was notified by a soldier that he had disappeared. Crook immediately informed Tibbles who guessed where Standing Bear was headed. So, Tibbles went in his own buggy to the Omaha reservation where he was loaned a horse and the services of a "young Indian." They traveled 120 miles in 18 hours until they finally caught up with Standing Bear on the banks of the Niobrara River. They convinced him to return to Fort Omaha before he was arrested. He agreed, still carrying the bones of Bear Shield in a sack around his neck - unburied.[353]

Standing Bear Makes Gifts

On May 18, 1879, Tibbles went to Fort Omaha to say goodbye to Standing Bear and the Poncas. Standing Bear took him out to a wildflower dotted hill on the western edge of the Fort, to speak with him.[354]

Gift to Thomas Tibbles (Beaded Buckskin Leggings). In his memoirs, Tibbles recorded that Standing Bear presented him a gift of his beaded buckskin leggings and told him he was a brother to him.[355]

Gift to John L. Webster (Tomahawk). The May 20, 1879, edition of the *Omaha Herald* told the story of Standing Bear coming into Omaha with Tibbles and Bright Eyes, to offer presents to his two attorneys. First, he went to Webster's home. After shaking hands, Standing Bear paid the following tribute to Webster:

> You and I are here. Our skins are of a different color, but God made us both. A little while ago when I was young, I was wild. I knew nothing of the ways of the white people. I see you have a nice house here. I look at these beautiful rooms. I would like to have a house too, and it may be after a while that I can get one, but not so good a house as this. That is what I want to do. For a great many years, a hundred years or more, the white men have been driving us about. They are shrewd, sharp and know how to cheat. But since I have been here, I have found them different. They have all treated me very kindly. I am very thankful for it. Hitherto when we have been wronged, we went to war. To assert our rights and avenge our wrongs we took the tomahawk. We had no law to punish those who did wrong, so we took our tomahawks and went to kill ... But you have found a better way. You have gone into the court for us and I find our wrongs can be righted there. Now I have no more use for the tomahawk. I want to lay it down forever. (here he stooped down, laid the tomahawk on the floor, and then stood erect and folded his arms and said:) I lay it down. I have no more use for it. I have found a better way. (then picking it up he handed it to Mr. Webster and said:) I present it to you as a token of my gratitude, that you may keep it in remembrance of this great victory you have gained. I have no further use for it. I can now seek the ways of peace.[356]

Gift to Andrew J. Poppleton (War Bonnet). After visiting Webster, Standing Bear went to the home of Andrew J. Poppleton. His wife, Caroline L. Poppleton, wrote an article dated January 5, 1915, describing Standing Bear's visit to their home that Sunday in late May:

> I remember in 1879 how Standing Bear with his interpreter called upon Mr. Poppleton at his rooms on the corner of Harney and Fifteenth where we boarded after our house on Capitol Hill was burned, to personally thank him for his speech on his behalf and with the War Bonnet in his hands, he offered it to Mr. Poppleton as his grateful act and his only pay for the words he had spoke for him and his tribe....Out of the poverty of his worldly possessions, he gave such visible token of his appreciation as he could, while out of the wealth of his human soul, and out of the fullness of his manly heart, he uttered sentiments, and expressed purposes which distinguish him as chief among ten thousand, and as a character, dark though his skin may be, altogether lovely.[357]

After this beautiful description of Standing Bear, Mrs. Poppleton shared Standing Bear's words as he gave the war bonnet (i.e. headdress) to Mr. Poppleton:

> I believe I told you in the court room, that God made me and that I was a man. For many years, we have been chased about, as a dog chases a wild beast. God sent you to help me. I thank you for what you have done. I want to get my land back. That is what I long for all the time. I wish to live there and be buried with my people. When you were speaking in the court room, of course I could not understand, but I could see that you were trying very hard to release me. I think you are doing for me and my people, something that never has been done before. If I had to pay you for it, I could never get enough to do it. I have here a relic which has come down to my people, through a great many generations. I do not know how

> old it is. It may be two or three hundred years old. I desire to present it to you for what you have done for me.[358]

Crook Releases His Prisoners

The May 17, 1879, edition of the *Omaha Herald* reported on the pending release of Standing Bear and the other Ponca prisoners and the generosity of Omaha residents to help them in their new life:

> Joseph LaFlesche (Iron Eye), the leading man among the Omahas, is in the city. He desires Standing Bear to locate on some land near the Omaha reservation which he thinks he can get for him and the Omaha will help him to get a start. It is proposed to donate provisions to supply them while on the journey. There are several sick in the band and he ought to have a little money for use on the way. Mr. L.S. Reed, on Fourteenth Street between Farnam and Douglas, will receive donations of food or money to be applied for this purpose. There are thirty persons in the party, many of them orphan children, whose parents died in the Indian Territory, and whom he is caring for as a matter of charity. No other case will ever appeal to the sympathy of an ever-generous Omaha public more strongly than this. Send around your donations to Mr. Reed and let us repair in some slight degree the great wrong which has been done to Standing Bear.[359]

On May 19, 1879, General George Crook loaded Standing Bear and his companions into wagons and had them escorted north to the largest of the islands in the Missouri River (considered by the Poncas as part of their traditional ancestral homeland), a few miles from the town of Niobrara, Nebraska. The island was hand-picked by Crook due to the fact that it was outside the boundaries of the Omaha Tribe and the Lakota Sioux, and yet on home ground. Somehow this island had not been included in the grant to the Sioux in the Fort Laramie Treaty of 1868. As soon as Standing Bear arrived on the island, he put his people to chop trees and build their new homes. The people of Niobrara welcomed their return and were pleased to help them.[360]

Bear Shield Buried

The traditional Ponca burial grounds were located on the bluffs near the Missouri River.[361] Journalism Professor Joe Starita described what happened a few months later when Standing Bear, his wife Susette, and other members of his family carried the bones of Bear Shield to his final resting place:

> They dug a fresh grave in the soil of their homeland. Honoring him with the full ceremonies of the tribe, the father laid Bear Shield's bones to rest, and said good-bye to his son.[362]

Omaha Ponca Relief Committee Created

Since Standing Bear's group had been legally declared separate from their tribe, the government was under no obligation to provide them with food, shelter, seed, tools or protection as provided by past treaties between the tribe and the government. Tibbles was determined to do something to help the Poncas. He made the rounds of his church connections and before long the Omaha Ponca Relief Committee was created. The founding members were:

Chair:	Robert Clarkson, Episcopal Bishop
Treasurer:	Alvin F. Sherrill, Congregational minister
Members:	James O'Connor, Catholic Bishop
	William Harsha, Presbyterian minister
	James W. Savage, Judge

In addition to helping the Poncas get settled in their new land with food, clothing, plows, pitchforks, lumber wagons, and seed, the Committee secured funds for future legal battles to be waged on behalf of the Ponca cause and to support Tibbles as he and others went East to enlist the support of influential men and women in the work ahead.[363]

The Four Head East

An important result of the Standing Bear decision was the mobilization of public opinion for Indian reform. This campaign gained momentum over the next two years through the speaking engagements of Thomas Tibbles, Standing Bear, Bright Eyes and her brother Woodworker (Francis LaFlesche). For the first time, American citizens in Chicago, Boston, New York, Philadelphia and Washington D.C. could listen to Standing Bear and Bright Eyes tell their story with eloquence and passion.[364]

One evening in late October 1879, the manager of the Boston hotel where the group was staying, gave Tibbles a telegram informing him that his wife Amelia had suddenly died back in Omaha. He went to his room and cried. Soon, Standing Bear came into his room and started praying and comforting the man he earlier called "my brother." They were joined by Francis LaFlesche who showed Tibbles a telegram Standing Bear had just received informing Standing Bear that his brother Big Snake was dead at the hands of government soldiers.[365] The two friends comforted each other in a time of mutual grief and agreed to stay the course and not abandon the tour.[366]

The group of four achieved its greatest notoriety in the City of Boston, where, as Francis Prucha noted, "a group of prominent men organized the Boston Indian Citizenship Committee to fight for the rights of the Poncas and other Indians… including the return to their original reservation."[367]

Newspaper reporters and editors, members of the clergy, and influential citizens took up the cause, including Delano A. Goddard, editor of the Boston Daily Advertiser, Massachusetts Senator Henry L. Dawes, poet Henry Wadsworth Longfellow, and muckraking journalist Helen Hunt Jackson.

Helen Hunt Jackson

Helen Hunt Jackson attended one of their talks in Boston. She was so energized that she put all her efforts for the next six years until her death in 1885 researching the story of the government's neglect of the Poncas and other Native American tribes. Her work titled *A Century of Dishonor* included hundreds of letters to congressmen, newspaper editors, and government officials, including Interior Secretary Carl Schurz.

During the East Coast tour, Thomas Tibbles's book, *The Ponca Chiefs*, was published. Bright Eyes wrote the introduction to the book, capturing the heart of the cause for justice:

> It is a little thing, a simple thing, which my people ask of a nation whose watchword is liberty; but it is endless in its consequences. They ask for their liberty, and law is liberty. For years the petitions of my people have gone up unnoticed, unheeded by all but their Creator, and now at last a man of your race has arisen, who has shown faith enough in humanity to arouse the nation from the sin of its indifference.[368]

As related in *The Indian Reform Letters of Helen Hunt Jackson,* edited by Valerie Sherer Mathes, Jackson wrote a letter on December 6, 1879 to her friend Whitelaw Reid, editor of the *New York Tribune*, telling him that Tibbles book would soon be published. Jackson related to Reid her conversation with Tibbles asking him where Bright Eyes came up with the phrase, "law is liberty". Tibbles replied that one evening when he entered their hotel room, he observed Bright Eyes looking out the window gazing upon men and women going in all directions as they pleased. Bright Eyes said to Tibbles, "that is being free; it is because they have law to take care of them that they can go."[369]

The Standing Bear case stirred the hearts of a number of people from all over the United States concerned about the injustice done to the Poncas. There may have been no one more affected or stirred to action than Helen Hunt Jackson. It became a crusade for her as evident by a letter she wrote on December 21, 1879 to Charles Dudley Warner, editor of the *Hartford Daily Courant,* saying, "I shall be found with 'Indians' engraved on my brain when I am dead. A fire has been kindled within me, which will never go out."[370]

Bright Eyes had developed a deep personal relationship with Helen Hunt Jackson so when Tibbles received the news Jackson had died in August 1885, he said that Bright Eyes cried and mourned the loss of her great friend for weeks. [371]

Senate Select Committee Report

Senator Henry Dawes (Massachusetts) chaired a United States Senate Select Committee in early 1880 to investigate "the circumstances of the removal of the Ponca Indians from their reservation." The committee called several witnesses to testify including, Thomas Tibbles, Standing Bear, Bright Eyes, White Eagle and Edward Kemble. The committee's 534-page report issued in May 1880, concluded:

> [T]his proceeding on the part of the United States was without justification and was a great wrong to this peaceable tribe of Indians and demands at the hands of the United States speedy and full redress.[372]

Susette LaFlesche Tibbles (Bright Eyes)
Courtesy of History Nebraska RG2026-05

Webster and Poppleton File Lawsuit

Nearly a year after the Standing Bear ruling, John Webster and Andrew Poppleton filed a lawsuit on April 3, 1880 in the Federal District Court of Nebraska, captioned *Ponca Tribe of Indians* (plaintiff) *v. Makh-pi-ah-lu-tah, or Red Cloud, in his own behalf and in behalf of the Sioux Tribe of Indians* (defendant). Judge Elmer S. Dundy ruled in favor of the plaintiffs on December 3, 1880 as reported in the *Omaha Daily Bee* newspaper for December 4, 1880:

> It was an action in ejectment instituted for the purpose of determining the title of the Poncas to the lands ceded to them by the United States under the Treaty of 1865 ... The pointed brief submitted for the Plaintiffs claims that if the Poncas acquired a title in fee simple, they had and still have a vested right in the lands, which cannot be divested by Congress, without their consent and upon adequate consideration. If, however, the right of the Poncas was only a right of occupancy, Congress had no right to divert the lands to other purposes, the right of the Poncas to occupancy being as sacred as that of the United States to the fee...Numerous authorities are cited in support of the Petition taken by the counsel for the Plaintiff. The Judgment of the court is as follows:
>
> That the Ponca Tribe of Indians, Plaintiff, has a legal estate in and is entitled to the possession of the real property described in the Petition, and that the Sioux Nation of Indians, unlawfully keeps it, the Ponca Tribe of Indians, out of the possession of the same, and the Court does access the damages of the Plaintiff by reason of the premises at the sum of $1. It is therefore ordered by the Court that the Plaintiff recover from the Defendant the real property described in the Petition, to-wit: all the islands lying in the Niobrara River and south of the middle of the main channel of said Niobrara River and within Townships 31 and 32 North and within Ranges 6, 7, 8, 9, and 10 West of the 6th Prime Meridian

of Kansas and Nebraska, and within the District and State of Nebraska.[373]

Ponca Commission Created

On December 18, 1880, President Rutherford B. Hayes appointed "The Ponca Commission" and tasked its members *"to ascertain the facts in regard to their removal and present condition, so far as was necessary to determine the question as to what justice and humanity require should be done by the Government of the United States."*[374]

The four members of the Ponca Commission were Brigadier General George Crook (Chairman), Brigadier General Nelson A. Miles, William Stickney, Secretary of the Board of Indian Commissioners, and Walter Allen of the Boston Indian Citizenship Committee. The commission took testimony from White Eagle and others at the Ponca Agency in Indian Territory, and then proceeded to Niobrara, Nebraska, where they heard the testimony of Standing Bear and his companions.[375]

Lieutenant John G. Bourke wrote in his diary that when the commission members and staff arrived in the Dakota village on January 11, 1881, to interview Standing Bear and other Poncas, the weather was bitter:

> The thermometer indicated -14 degrees. Snow lay to a great depth, in level places 12-14 inches, in drifts of at least 5 ft. Crossing the Niobrara river to a large island, we reached the village of the Poncas - consisting of both tepis and log-houses. The Chief Standing Bear and his brother, Yellow Horse, and the old chief Smoke Maker and several others came up to shake hands.... The Poncas have ponies, wagons, cattle, hogs, hay and wood piles and other indications of thrift and increasing comfort. A supply of blankets had just reached them from friends in Omaha, Nebraska which they were engaged in distributing among their women and children. This year, they have cultivated over 100 acres of corn, which is stored in granaries and have been, with the exception of some little assistance

> from sympathizing friends in Boston and Omaha, independent of outside help.[376]

Later that day, the commission members heard the testimony of Standing Bear:

> My children have been exterminated; my brother has been killed.... But they can't scare me, drive me into a bad hole yet. I have come back to my own land....I was brought up before the court and it released me....I am living back on my old land, that I am doing well there, and that I am working for myself....I do not wish to go elsewhere....Whatever damages are coming to us, and whatever annuities, I want them to be split in two, one part for us Poncas here, and one part for the Poncas in Indian Territory. I desire you to help me in this. I don't want an agent. I want to have a teacher or a minister. I want a missionary to be with me, and to attend to me.[377]

The commission made its report to President Hayes on January 26, 1881. It described the incredible ineptitude, indifference, and mismanagement that had made the experience of the Poncas needlessly disastrous and cruel, making the following conclusions:

> That the removal of the Ponca Indians from their reservation in Dakota and Nebraska, where they were living by virtue of treaties made with the United States of 1858 and 1865, was not only most unfortunate for the Indians, resulting in great hardships and serious loss of life and property, but was injudicious and without sufficient cause. It was also without lawful authority, inasmuch as the law requiring the consent of the Indians as a condition precedent to their removal was overlooked or wholly disregarded.
>
> That the lands from which the Poncas were removed had been ceded and relinquished to them by the United States for ample consideration specified in the treaties. That the

> government solemnly covenanted not only to warrant and defend their title to these lands, but also to protect their persons and property thereon. That the Indians had violated no condition of the treaty by which their title to the lands or claims to protection had been forfeited, and that this rightful claim still exists in full force and effect, notwithstanding all acts done by the government of the United States.
>
> That the Indians who have returned to their reservation in Dakota have the strongest possible attachment to their lands and a resolute purpose to retain them. They have received no assistance from the government and except the limited aid furnished by benevolent people, they have been entirely self-sustaining. With few agricultural implements they have cultivated a considerable tract of land for their support. They are on friendly terms with all other Indian Tribes, including the Sioux, as well as with the white settlers in their vicinity. They pray that they may not again be disturbed.[378]

The commission recommended the Poncas be given an allotment of land on their former reservation, an appropriation of money "for agricultural implements, stock, seed, and construction of comfortable dwellings and a schoolhouse," and that "all Indians should have the opportunity of appealing to the courts for the protection and vindication of their rights of person and property."[379]

The commission report was certified on January 25, 1881 by John G. Bourke, First Lieutenant, Third Cavalry, Aide-de-Camp, U.S. Army.

Land Allotments to the Poncas

Following the recommendations of the Ponca Commission, Congress made an appropriation of $165,000 on March 3, 1881, to indemnify the Ponca tribe for losses sustained in consequence of the removal, and to declare their right to go back onto their old homeland. The appropriation was to be made as follows:

1) To the Southern Poncas $50,000 to buy 101,000 acres from the Cherokees; $20,000 to buy livestock and as cash stipends.

2) To the Northern Poncas $10,000 cash stipends, $5000 for building, $5000 for education, $5000 for livestock, seed and other farming products.

3) $70,000 to be placed into a trust fund to earn 5% interest to be split among all Poncas equally on an annual basis.[380]

In the summer of 1881, Samuel J. Kirkwood, newly appointed Secretary of the Interior, replacing Carl Schurz, met with representatives of the Lakota Sioux and Ponca Tribes in Washington D.C. The parties reached an agreement whereby the Lakota Sioux ceded to the Poncas some 26,000 acres of the original 96,000 acres which the government had through a "clerical error" taken from the Poncas in the Fort Laramie Treaty of 1868.[381]

In 1887, Congress passed a General Allotment Act, known as the Dawes Severalty Act ("The Dawes Act"). Each Indian head of household was granted an allotment of reservation land. In August 1890, Standing Bear and the nearly 200 Poncas who had returned to the old reservation received their allotment. By 1891, a total of 27,202 acres had been allotted to 167 heads of families and single adults."[382]

The Dawes Act allotted up to 320 acres for each head of a family, up to 160 acres for a single adult, up to 160 acres for minors who were orphans, and up to 80 acres for all other minors. The allotment to Standing Bear was nearly 300 acres located near the river.

Some historians believe the allotment legislation, specifically the Dawes Act, had a different and sometimes negative result for the tribes than anticipated when it was enacted.[383]

By 1890, the population of the Ponca Tribe seemed to have been restored to its size at the time of the forced removal. A government report issued in 1890 estimated that there were 217 Poncas living in the Nebraska region, while 605 Poncas were living in Indian Territory.[384]

Standing Bear & Family on His Own Allotted Land, 1903
Courtesy of History Nebraska RG 2039-08

Standing Bear with Family, Home and Gardens, 1903
Courtesy of History Nebraska RG 2039-09

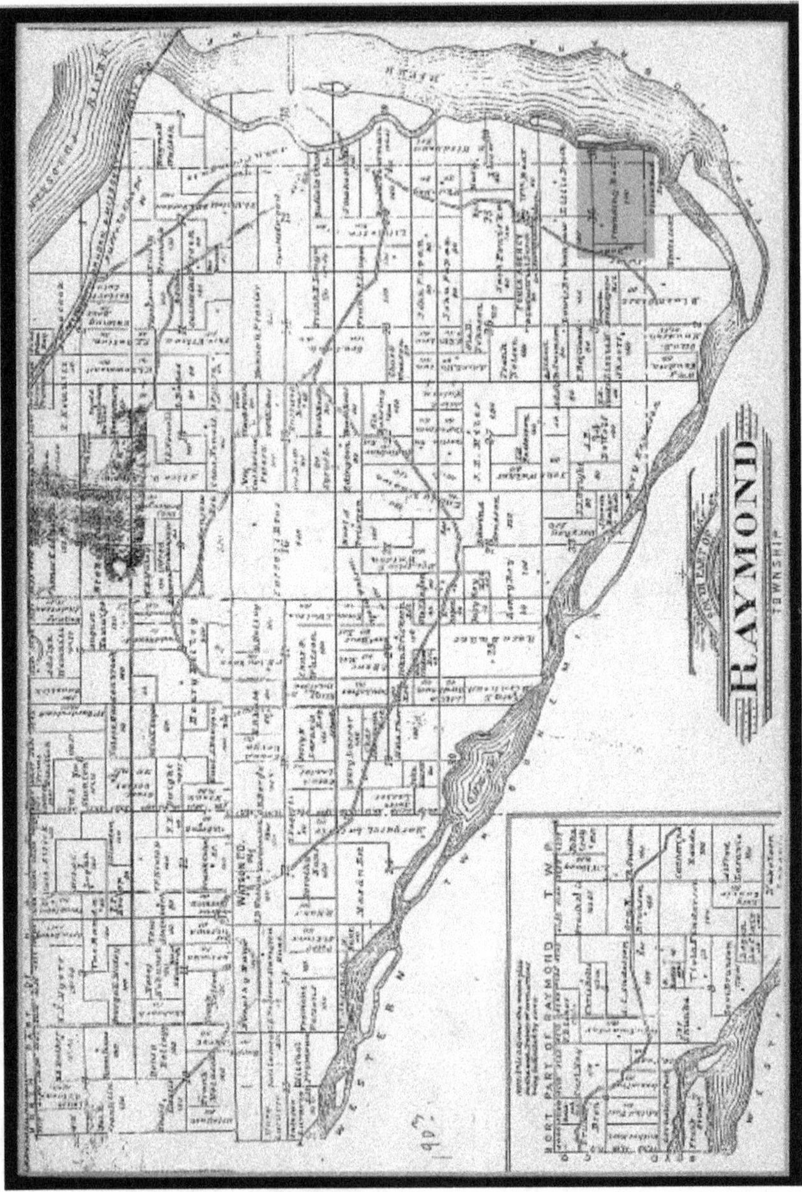

Ponca Homeland in Nebraska (1903)

Standing Bear's allotment (top right shaded), Otto Kundson's allotment (grandfather of Judi gaiashkibos), south of Standing Bear's land

Courtsey of Judi gaiashkibos, Executive Director, Nebraska Commission on Indian Affairs.

Chapter 19

Impact of Decision in Later Cases

The Standing Bear decision has been cited in various courts in the United States including: United States Supreme Court (1884); Supreme Court of Wisconsin (1910), United States Board of Tax Appeals (1926), United States Court of Appeals Second Circuit (1996), United States Court of Appeals Ninth Circuit (2005), and the United States District Court of Utah (2009).[385]

Definition of "Person"

The Standing Bear decision has been cited as authority for the definition of the word "person:"

> The word "person" as it is ordinarily used means a living human being. It is so defined in Webster's and in Johnson's and in the Century Dictionaries. It is so defined by the courts, **U.S. v. Crook, 25 Fed. Case. 695.** *State Ex.Rel. Bancroft v. Frear, Secretary of State*, Supreme Court of Wisconsin, 128 N.W. 1068 (1910).
>
> The Indian was a person irrespective of citizenship. **United States ex.rel Standing Bear v. Crook**. (*Appeal of Leah Brunt, Administratix, Estate of Theodore S. Brunt*, United States Board of Tax Appeals, 5 B.T.A. (1926)

Nature and Scope of Evidence Required

The Standing Bear decision has been cited as authority in determining the nature and scope of evidence a court required to decide whether a Native American severed ties with a tribe:

In the famous case of **United States ex. rel. Standing Bear v. Crook** in which an Indian secured a writ of habeas corpus directed against a general of the Unites States Army, to prevent his removal to Indian Territory, Standing Bear had severed his relationship with his tribe and was therefore, not subject to the provisions of any treaties or legislation concerned with the removal of the tribe to Indian Territory. In reaching that conclusion, the court opined, in the tone of the day, that "the individual Indian possesses the clear and God-given right to withdraw from his tribe." *Dana Leigh Thompson v. County of Franklin,* United States District Court of the State of New York, 180 F.R.D. 216 (1998).

Tribal membership is a bilateral relation, depending for its existence not only upon the action of the Tribe but also the action of the individual concerned. Any member of any Indian tribe is at full liberty to terminate his tribal relationship whenever he so chooses. (Felix S. Cohen, Handbook of Federal Indian Law, 22 (1982Ed.), (cited in Thompson v. County of Franklin, 180 F.R.D. 216, 225 (N.D.N.Y. 1998). A member of an Indian tribe "possesses the clear and God given right to withdraw from his tribe and forever live away from it as though it had not further existence." **United States ex. Rel. Standing Bear v. Crook,** 25 F. Cas. 695,649 (Circ.Ct. D.Neb.1879). *In the Matter of the Adoption of C.D.K., a Minor Child*, United States District Court of Utah, 2009 WL 2494618 (2009).

Impact on Issue of Citizenship

John Elk, a Winnebago, severed his relations with his tribe and lived with a white family in Omaha. On April 5, 1880 Elk went to the voting registration office for the Fifth Ward asking to register to vote in the upcoming City election. Charles Wilkins, registrar for the Fifth Ward, refused to allow him to register since he was an Indian and therefore not a citizen.

John L. Webster and Andrew J. Poppleton filed suit on behalf of John Elk in the Federal Circuit Court in Omaha, Nebraska. The case of *Elk v. Wilkins* was heard before Circuit Court Justices Elmer S. Dundy and George McCrary. The defendant, Charles Wilkins, was represented by Federal District Attorney Genio M. Lambertson.

The District Attorney filed a demurrer citing Plaintiff's failure to state a proper cause of action because only citizens could vote in a Nebraska election, therefore, the court was without jurisdiction to hear this matter. The two judges concurred and dismissed the case. Webster and Poppleton filed an appeal to the United States Supreme Court.[386]

Professors John R. Wunder and Mark R. Scherer explain how Judge Dundy, a district court judge, could sit on the Elk case as a circuit court judge:

> In 1869 congress passed 'An Act to amend the Judicial System of the United States.' This revision of the lower federal courts began the process of creating the modern appellate division, but it would take nearly forty years to straighten things out...This new structural arrangement also meant that Elmer Dundy was now for all practical purposes both the district court judge and the circuit court judge for the State of Nebraska....The case was heard before the circuit court that included Judge Dundy and George Washington McCrary...McCrary served with Judge Dundy on the circuit court from 1879 to 1884.... The *Elk v. Wilkins* trial was heard before Judge Dundy in Omaha. Dundy kept McCrary, who remained in Iowa, posted on developments.[387]

In 1884, the United States Supreme Court affirmed the lower court's decision against John Elk, ruling:

> Upon the question whether any action of a state can confer rights of citizenship on Indians of a tribe still recognized by the United States as retaining its tribal

> existence, we need not, and do not, express an opinion, because the State of Nebraska is not shown to have taken any action affecting the condition of the plaintiff. The Plaintiff, not being a citizen of the United States under the fourteenth amendment of the constitution, has been deprived of no right secured by the fifteenth amendment, and cannot maintain this action. Judgment affirmed.[388]

The Elks case is important for two reasons. First, it is evident that the Standing Bear decision emboldened Elk, Webster and Poppleton to file suit in a federal court to test the issue of citizenship. The Elk case proved that an individual Native American who had severed his ties with his tribe could have his day in court, seeking redress of his grievances. Within five years of the Standing Bear decision, John Elk, a Native American, had his case heard before the United States Supreme Court.

Secondly, the case is also important for being one of the first times in which Justice John M. Harlan gave a dissenting opinion. President Hayes appointed Harlan to the Supreme Court. Within a few years of his appointment, Justice Harlan issued a number of dissents in cases restricting civil freedoms; including his famous dissent in the 1896 case of *Plessy v. Ferguson* (163 U.S. 537) which upheld the practice of segregation of railroads under the doctrine of "separate but equal." Known as "The Great Dissenter," Justice Harlan's dissenting opinion in the Elk case stated:

> Born therefore, in the territory, under the dominion and within the jurisdictional limits of the United States, plaintiff has acquired, as was his undoubted right, a residence in one of the states, with her consent, and is subject to taxation and to all other burdens imposed by her upon residents of every race. If he did not acquire national citizenship on abandoning his tribe and becoming, by resident in one of the states, subject to the complete jurisdiction of the United States, then the Fourteenth Amendment has wholly failed to accomplish, in respect of the Indian race, what, we think, was

> intended by it; and there is still in this country a despised and rejected class of persons with no nationality whatever, who, born in our territory, owing no allegiance to any foreign power, and subject, as residents of the states, to all the burdens of government, are yet not members of any political community, nor entitled to any of the rights, privileges, or immunities of citizens of the United States.[389]

In 1885, the Board of Indian Commissioners issued a strong declaration on the subject of citizenship:

> For what ought we to hope as the future of the Indian? To this there is one answer - and but one. He should become an intelligent citizen of the United States.[390]

The expressed desire of so many people to grant citizenship to Native Americans was finally achieved in 1924 with the passage of The Indian Freedom Citizenship Suffrage Act, known as *the Snyder Act.* It was named after its chief sponsor, Representative Homer P. Snyder of New York. The Snyder Act reads:

> Be it enacted by the Senate and House of Representatives of the United States of America in Congress assembled, that all non-citizen Indians born in the territorial limits of the United States be, and they are hereby, declared to be citizens of the United States: Provided, that the granting of such citizenship shall not in any manner impair or otherwise affect the right of any Indian to tribal or other property.[391]

It was not until 1948, "that the last two states, Arizona and New Mexico, finally granted the franchise to the Indians of their states." [392]

Note: The United States Supreme Court's first interpretation of the Fourteenth Amendment regarding citizenship was in the Slaughter-House Cases. The case is especially noted for a dissent given by Justice Stephen J. Field. [393]

Summary

The Standing Bear decision impacted various court decisions throughout the United States. It laid the foundation for Native Americans to file petitions in federal courts seeking redress for their grievances. As "persons" in the eyes of the law, they now had "standing to sue" for the first time in American history. The historic decision was the first step in the civil rights journey of Native Americans for equality under the American legal system. The journey would be long. More suffering would be endured, and setbacks would occur. But the foundation had been laid.

The journey for justice had begun.

Chapter 20

The Omaha Connection

History is primarily a story of people who become connected to each other through a common purpose, event or person. Their relationship may be short term or last for years. Some relationships change the course of history, as happened in this case.

"But For"[394] the courage, commitment and kindness of a small group of people, this story would have had a very different and unfavorable ending for Standing Bear and his companions:

The People of Omaha, Nebraska
Thomas Tibbles (newspaper reporter)
Bright Eyes (interpreter)
John Webster (lawyer)
Andrew Poppleton (lawyer)
Iron Eye (chief of the Omaha tribe)
Elmer S. Dundy (judge)
George Crook (U.S. Army general)

Standing Bear and the plight of the Poncas attracted this small group of people who came together from diverse economic, social, religious and political backgrounds for the purpose of bringing justice to an unjust situation. They became connected not for monetary enrichment or personal ambition, but because in their heart they knew a terrible wrong had been committed that needed to be rectified. It needed to be accomplished through words and deeds, not weapons. Justice demanded nothing less. Together, this small group made history.

So, we might ask, "What happened to this group after the Trial was over?"

The People of Omaha

The People of Omaha deserve special recognition for their support of Standing Bear and the Ponca prisoners. They packed the courtroom for the trial, cheered the ruling, and organized the Ponca Relief Committee to support the Poncas with food, supplies and money for their journey home. The *Omaha Herald* newspaper publicized the Ponca story and gained valuable support for reform around the nation. Omaha clergy from various Christian denominations and faiths provided moral encouragement and leadership as well. The small Jewish community also contributed financial support to the fund to help defray future litigation costs on behalf of the Poncas.

Thomas Tibbles (1840-1928) and Bright Eyes (1854-1903)

Thomas Tibbles said that the first time he heard Bright Eyes speak after the Standing Bear Trial was in an Omaha church, in the fall of 1879. She was small in size, but graceful and dignified in her bearing. He could sense she was frightened, yet she composed herself and spoke clearly, as she described some of the horrors endured by Standing Bear and his family having their land taken from them and suffering through the deaths of two of their children. Bright Eyes became so moved by the story she was sharing, as well as by the intensity of the audience reaction, that she nearly fainted. People on the platform grabbed hold of her before she fell and helped her outside. Tibbles said the way in which she delivered her talk "thrilled the audience like an electric shock."[395]

In the fall of 1879, Tibbles and Bright Eyes were introduced to ethnologist Alice C. Fletcher in Boston. Two years later they led her on a tour of the Ponca and Omaha villages. Standing Bear met Fletcher on his homeland. Fletcher spent the next 20 years studying the culture of these two tribes. In 1911, she published her work with Francis LaFlesche.[396]

Tibbles and Bright Eyes toured England and Scotland in addition to the eastern states of America. On June 29, 1882, in the Presbyterian Mission Church on the Omaha Reservation, Thomas Tibbles, age 42, and Bright Eyes, age 27, were married. They worked tirelessly together on behalf of various Ponca and Omaha tribal causes for 21 years until her death, even testifying before congressional committees, 1879-1882.[397]

In the beginning of their marriage, they lived in Tibbles home in Omaha with his two children, Eda and May, by his first marriage to Amelia Tibbles. Then in 1883, they farmed a quarter section of land near Bancroft, Nebraska. Bright Eyes wrote a number of articles on Indian life for national magazines. They moved to Washington D.C. in 1893 working as newspaper correspondents for *The Nonconformist*, an Indiana weekly paper, as well as for *The Farmers' Alliance.*

Tibble's Family Home in Bancroft, NE, Thomas (seated on left) Susette (seated in upper window). Two women may be Tibbles daughters Eda and May (near front door)
Courtesy History Nebraska RG2026-47

In the last years of her life, Bright Eyes became an accomplished painter, even illustrating a book about life in the Omaha tribe written by a friend. At the young age of 49, Bright Eyes died on May 26, 1903. She is buried in a cemetery in Bancroft, Nebraska near her parents.[398] In 1983, she was inducted in the Nebraska Hall of Fame.

Outdoor Dining
Thomas Tibbles & Susette LaFlesche Tibbles
Omaha Tribe agency, August 1901
(their backs are to the photographer,
family dog behind Tibbles's chair)
Courtesy of History Nebraska RG 2737-13

After her death, Tibbles continued his work for various newspapers in Nebraska, including the Omaha World Herald (successor to the *Omaha Herald*), and The Independent, a weekly Populist Party newspaper. He became so active in Populist Party politics, that he was chosen as the Vice-Presidential candidate on the national Populist Party ticket in 1904.[399] [400]

Tibbles wrote his autobiography *Buckskin and Blanket Days* in 1905. In 1907, he married Ida Belle Riddle. They remained together until his death in Omaha on May 14, 1928, at age 88.

Thomas Tibbles in his Study (1908) with His Dog
Courtesy of History Nebraska RG2737-05

John L. Webster (1847-1929)

One of the most distinguished lawyers in Nebraska history, John L. Webster served as Omaha city attorney, general counsel for the Omaha Water Board, the Council Bluffs Street Railway Co. and the Wabash Railroad. He argued rates cases before the Interstate Commerce Commission in Washington D.C. and the United States Supreme Court. In 1903, he was elected president of the Nebraska Bar Association.[401]

Webster was active in Republican Party politics. He was chosen as a delegate to the Republican National conventions in 1892 and 1896, and in the process, became friends with President William McKinley.[402]

Webster was also very active in the Omaha community serving in a variety of leadership positions including director of the Trans-Mississippi Exposition, Omaha's version of a World's Fair, in 1898. His friendship with William McKinley was instrumental in bringing the President to the Exposition. He served as a director of the Omaha Library Board alongside A.J. Poppleton, as president of the Nebraska Historical Society, and as founder of The Friends of Art Association in Nebraska. He was a great patron of the arts, bringing fine paintings to Omaha from his European travels. The civic and philanthropic organization known as Ak-Sar-Ben (Nebraska spelled backwards) honored him as their "King" in 1916 for over 60 years of civic and legal service to the community. A street is named after him in Omaha. John L. Webster died on September 2, 1929, at age 82. He is buried in Forest Lawn Cemetery, Omaha.[403]

Andrew J. Poppleton (1830-1896)

In his memoirs, *Reminiscences,* Andrew J. Poppleton wrote that he filed the first lawsuit ever tried in the State of Nebraska, *John Pentecost v. F. M. Woods,* which concerned a land dispute on a tributary of Saddle Creek near present-day Elmwood Park in Omaha. Due to the fact that his early law practice consisted mainly of trials of land claims, he founded the Omaha Claim Club, a tribunal seeking to protect the claims of original landowners against "claim-jumpers." Poppleton continued serving as general counsel for the Union Pacific Railroad until 1888, and he appeared as co-counsel with John Webster on a few other cases filed in court on behalf of the Poncas and other Native Americans. Poppleton was active in Democratic Party politics, having been its nominee for the United States Senate in 1867, and for the United States House of Representatives in 1868. He lost both elections.

Poppleton served as Omaha's second mayor in 1858. He became active in real estate development in Omaha. The Poppleton Block was built by him in 1886 and is today listed on the National Register of Historic Places. Like Webster, a street in Omaha is named after Poppleton. Since he had grown up on a farm in Michigan, he purchased some 1200 acres of land near Elkhorn, Nebraska, and raised trotting horses. *Reminiscences* ends with Poppleton writing, "About the first of July 1892, I became totally blind. My life of light was ended, and my life of darkness began."[404] He died on September 9, 1896 and is buried in Prospect Hill Cemetery in Omaha.

Iron Eye (1822-1888)

Iron Eye (Joseph LaFlesche) was half-Native American and half-French. He was the last Chief of the Omaha Tribe. He had seven children: Marguerite, Lucy, Noah, Carey, Francis (Woodworker), Susette (Bright Eyes), and Susan LaFlesche Picotte, the first Native American physician. Iron Eye was a leader in the effort to provide financial support and supplies to the Poncas after their release. Without his courage in risking arrest by riding to Fort Omaha to inform General Crook of the Poncas story, their outcome would likely have been very different. Iron Eye died on September 24, 1888, at age 67. He is buried in the Cemetery in Bancroft, Nebraska next to his wife, Mary Gale.[405]

Elmer S. Dundy (1830-1896)

Judge Elmer S. Dundy served on the Territorial Supreme Court from 1863 to 1867 when Nebraska was granted statehood. He was Nebraska's first United States district judge. "He presided over Nebraska's federal bench from May 1868 until his death on October 28, 1896, a twenty-eight-year period that defined Nebraska's first era of its federal judiciary."[406] His ruling in the Standing Bear case was courageous and monumental to the Native American reform movement. He is buried in the Moravian Cemetery in Staten Island, New York. A county in Western Nebraska is named in his honor.

George Crook (1828-1890)

Lieutenant John G. Bourke recorded in his diary a letter that General George Crook wrote from his office at Fort Omaha to Thomas Tibbles. The letter was dated June 19, 1879, nearly seven weeks after the Standing Bear Trial. The letter shows clearly the heart and soul of General Crook as he relates strong feelings for the wrongs committed against Native Americans and the correct policy he hoped would be pursued in the future on their behalf:

> It seems to me to be an odd feature of our judicial system that the only people in this country who have no rights under the law are the original owners of the soil....The true and only policy to pursue with the Indian is to treat him just as we treat a white man.[407]

General Crook left Omaha in 1882 for assignment as Commander of the Department of Arizona. Four years later, he was reassigned to Omaha as Commander of the Department of the Platte. In 1888, he was elevated to the rank of Major General of the Army and assigned as Commander of the Division of the Missouri stationed in Chicago. He served a total of nine years at Fort Omaha (1875-82 and 1886-88).[408]

General George Crook died on March 21, 1890 at the age of 62. He is buried in Arlington National Cemetery. Former

President Rutherford B. Hayes was a pallbearer at his funeral. Red Cloud, Chief of the Ogallala Sioux, gave a fitting tribute: "He, at least, had never lied to us. His words gave us hope."[409]

These Omaha men and women came together before and after the trial to support Standing Bear and the Ponca cause.

But, there was only one leading man – One Hero!

Chapter 21

Standing Bear
(1829-1908)

This is a story of a leading man. This is the story of a great and noble man. A man of courage and determination who was willing to face arrest for leaving the government's reservation without its permission, all because of his love for his son and his people.

Standing Bear is the hero of this story.

Standing Bear was a man who fought for his freedom, not with armed resistance, but with bold action, strong testimony and heartfelt eloquence. He knew he and his people had been wronged. All he wanted was the right to live and die with his family on his own land - on the beloved land of his Ponca ancestors.

This story is a civil rights victory for Native Americans, unprecedented in American history. For the first time, a federal court declared a Native American to be a "person" – a human being, having rights and privileges to file an action for a redress of grievances in a federal court, like every other person in America.

Standing Bear won his fight for freedom. His victory began a movement of change, a slow change, but a change, nevertheless. The pervading sense of indifference toward Native Americans, which was lamented by Bright Eyes, was broken.[410] America would never be the same because of what Standing Bear did.

Everything had been taken from him, except his pride in being a Ponca. He carried the stories in his heart of the ancestors gone before him and their love of the land they called home for over 200 years.

Standing Bear built a new home for his family on the nearly 300 acres allotted to him by the government. He fenced his pasture for cattle. He raised corn, wheat, squash, beans and potatoes. He lived his last years surrounded by his wife Susette and her niece Lottie, and their children and grandchildren on the land he loved, as he had always dreamed.

Standing Bear died on September 3, 1908.
He was 79 years of age.

He had achieved all he had ever wanted:

To live on his own land

To be buried on his own land

To live and die a free man

Chief Standing Bear (1877)
Courtesy of History Nebraska RG1227-02-02

Chapter 21 - Standing Bear

Epilogue

In 1946 Congress organized the Indian Claims Commission and gave each of the dispossessed Indian Tribes five years to organize and lodge their formal claims seeking justice for loss of their homelands. Professor David Wishart noted the Ponca received satisfaction for their claims in 1972:

> *Docket 322* involved the 1858 cession of Ponca land. They "were awarded $1,878,500 representing the difference between what they were originally paid (19.5 cents per acre) and what they should have been paid ($1.00 per acre)."[411]
>
> *Docket 323* involved the 1877 removal of the Poncas to Indian Territory. They "were granted the difference between the consideration and the fair market value of the land ($174,327), but allotted 5% interest a year on the principal, because the taking had been without consent. By the time of the final judgment in 1972, the award had accumulated to $1,013,425." [412] [413]

Those members of the Poncas who remained in Indian Territory for a variety of reasons are known today as the Southern Poncas (the "Maste-Pa-ca" or "Hot Country Poncas").[414]

Those members of the Poncas who later came back to the Nebraska region to join Standing Bear and his group are known today as the Northern Poncas (the "Osni Pa Ca" or "Cold Country Poncas").

The Ponca Tribe was terminated by the government in 1966, along with a number of other tribes throughout the nation. The remaining land held by the tribe in Nebraska was distributed to its members. But the desire of tribal members to preserve their unique culture and traditions for themselves and future generations led them to pursue congressional support to restore their tribal status. The Ponca Restoration Act was signed by the President in 1990. Today, the official name of the tribe is "The Ponca Tribe of Nebraska."

The Ponca Tribe of Nebraska provides health, education, social and cultural services and resources to its members in a "Service Delivery Area" consisting of 15 counties within Nebraska, Iowa and South Dakota. The tribe does not have a reservation.[415]

A Fitting Tribute

As a fitting tribute, the Nebraska Legislature commissioned Artist Benjamin Victor to create a sculpture of Ponca Chief Standing Bear as one of two sculptures representing the State of Nebraska in Statuary Hall at the United States Capitol in Washington D.C. The dedication took place on September 18, 2019.[416]

Author's Note

I have lived all of my life in Omaha, where the Standing Bear Trial took place. My ancestors immigrated from Tipperary, Ireland, in 1875 to work for the Union Pacific Railroad. They lived less than twelve blocks from the federal courthouse. I often wondered why they came directly to Omaha. In researching this book, I discovered a possible answer. The Nebraska Legislature created a Board of Immigration in 1870 for the specific purpose of advertising "in this county or in foreign countries" for workers to come to Omaha.[417]

My great-grandfather, Patrick Joseph Dwyer, likely read the advertisement and came to Omaha to work as a finish carpenter for the Union Pacific Railroad. Recently, I discovered a treasure in the basement of our family home which has been preserved for more than 140 years: *Wolfe's Omaha City Directory for 1878-79.* In the year of the Standing Bear trial, the Directory listed my great-grandfather as "P.J. Dwyer, carpenter UPRR, 215 Capitol Ave."[418]

I wonder whether any of my ancestors knew the participants in the Standing Bear trial or attended the court proceedings. Was the case talked about at their evening meals? The City Directory shows that Tibbles, Webster, Poppleton, Crook, and the clergy lived within a few blocks of each other and of my family.[419]

American and British History was my major at the University of Nebraska-Omaha. Yet, the textbook used in a special course on the History of Nebraska, which I still possess, devotes only a few pages to the history of the Poncas, and less than one page to the Standing Bear Trial itself.[420]

My knowledge of this case was greatly enhanced in 2009, when I was a member of the Board of Directors of the Douglas County Historical Society. The Society's headquarters are in the Crook House on the grounds of the old Fort Omaha. Our board meetings took place in General Crooks' dining room. In an adjacent room was his office where he held his historic interview with Standing Bear during his imprisonment.

Union Pacific Railroad Yards
8th-10th Streets & Forest Ave., Omaha
Looking East in 1875, the year the author's great-grandfather came to Omaha from Ireland to work for the Railroad at this location, at the open-air building, known as the "Cowshed."
Courtesy from the Bostwick-Frohardt Collection, owned by KM3TV and on permanent loan to The Durham Museum Omaha, BF31-351-04A

Union Pacific Railroad Yards
8th-10th Streets & Forest Ave., Omaha
Looking North in 1876, "Cowshed" on right
Courtesy from the Bostwick-Frohardt Collection, owned by KM3TV and on permanent loan to The Durham Museum Omaha, BF14-66

In May 2009, efforts were underway to commemorate the 130th anniversary of the Standing Bear trial via a series of events. Betty Davis, then executive director of the Douglas County Historical Society, requested I make some remarks about the trial from a lawyer's perspective.

On the day of the Society's commemoration of the trial, I listened with interest and admiration to the other presenters. The talk given by Joe Starita, Professor of Journalism at the University of Nebraska-Lincoln, based on his book, *"I Am A Man"* was captivating. His subsequent lectures further inspired me to write this book.

I am also grateful to those who attended the 2009 event and encouraged me to write a book looking at the case from a lawyer's point of view. For the past ten years, I have researched many primary source materials including the treaties the Poncas signed with the government, pertinent federal cases, government reports, congressional legislation, ethnology studies, newspaper accounts of the day, and much more, in an effort to verify the facts as much as possible.

I am awed by Standing Bear. He was an eloquent speaker and poet; a man of courage and integrity. Above all, he was a loving and devoted husband, father, grandfather, and friend. I feel very privileged to have spent ten years getting to know and appreciate this great man.

The atmosphere in the Omaha courtroom those first two days of May 1879 must have been electric. I feel it even today. I hope you did as well.

Omaha in the 1870's

View NW from 15th & Douglas Street
Federal Court Office, under construction (middle right)
Courtesy from The Bostwick-Frohardt Collection owned by KM3TV and on permanent loan to The Durham Museum, Omaha. BF14-385-420E.

Omaha in the 1870's

View NW from 14th & Farnam Street
Facing Capitol Hill
Courtesy from The Bostwick-Frohardt Collection owned by KM3TV and on permanent loan to The Durham Museum, Omaha. BF14-020A

Chapter Discussion Questions For Students and Book Clubs

Prologue and Chapter One

1. In your opinion, what three attributes best describe Standing Bear based on the Prologue?

2. What do the words of Lieutenant Bourke in Chapter One add to your understanding of Standing Bear?

3. After viewing the photograph of Standing Bear in Chapter One, describe your impression of his persona.

Chapter Two

4. Why would the Poncas decide to settle in the Niobrara River valley?

5. Describe the importance of ancestral land to the Poncas.

6. What information did the "Notable Visitors" add to the portrayal of the Ponca tribe?

Chapter Three

7. How does the meaning of the word "law" apply to the Ponca's self-governance?

8. What is the basis of the Ponca's System of Law?

9. Describe the purpose of the Sacred Pipe in Ponca society. Do we have anything comparable today?

10. How does the Ponca legal process and penalties for breaking a rule of conduct reflect the respect they have for each other and the common good of the tribe?

Chapter Four

11. How did Justice Marshall justify the "doctrine of discovery?"

12. What effect did Justice Marshall's ruling that Native Americans were "wards of the government" have on the Poncas?

13. What negative impact did the additional acts of Congress have on the Poncas?

Chapter Five

14. What was the principle behind the Northwest Ordinance and how did Justice Marshall ignore it in the *Johnson* and *Cherokee* rulings?

15. In your opinion what importance should be given to Article VI of the U.S. Constitution in the treaty-making process with Native American tribes?

16. Describe the tragic consequences of the Ponca Treaty of 1858.

17. Why do you think the word "blunder" is associated with the 1868 Sioux Treaty at Fort Laramie?

18. The Northwest Ordinance established the principle of "good faith" in government dealings with Native American tribes. How did this ordinance fail to be applied to the Poncas?

19. Why were the Poncas at a disadvantage in negotiating treaties with the government?

Chapter Six

20. What impact did the vanishing of the buffalo have on the Great Plains tribes?

21. How did Inspector Kemble persuade the Ponca chiefs to go with him to Indian Territory?

22. Why did Inspector Kemble abandon the chiefs in Indian Territory and how did they react?

23. Describe the first time Standing Bear was arrested.

24. What finding did the Senate Select Committee on the Ponca Removal issue in 1880 concerning this episode?

Chapter Seven

25. Describe your feelings when you hear Standing Bear itemize the loss of his property?

26. How long did the Journey of Sorrows take?

27. What types of suffering did the Poncas endure during the journey?

28. What was the condition of the Ponca people when the chiefs returned to Indian Territory after their visit with President Hayes?

Chapter Eight

29. If you were a farmer at that time and you saw these pitiful people come your way in the middle of winter, would you help them?

30. If you were among the Ponca tribe and walked all the way to Indian Territory in Oklahoma, how would you feel?

Chapter Nine

31. Describe the relationship between General Crook and Thomas Tibbles and why it was so important to this story.

32. What motivated Chief Iron Eye and his daughter Bright Eyes to risk arrest in order to visit General Crook?

Chapter Ten

33. How would you describe the attitude of the Ponca prisoners during their interview by Tibbles?

34. What motivated General Crook to invite the Ponca prisoners into his office for a formal interview?

35. After the two interviews were over, why would Tibbles first action be to visit Omaha churches?

36. What effect did the Tibbles April 1, 1879 *Omaha Herald* article have on local and national interest in the Ponca prisoners?

Chapter Eleven

37. If you had been a lawyer in Omaha, would you have refused the plea made by Thomas Tibbles to help the Poncas? If so, why?

38. What factors would you as a lawyer consider before making a decision to help the Poncas or not?

Chapter Twelve

39. How would you describe the purpose of the Writ of Habeas Corpus?

40. Is there any connection between the Writ and the newly enacted 14th Amendment to the Constitution?

41. When Judge Dundy issued the Writ, how did the government react?

Chapter Thirteen

42. What would you have felt if you had been sitting in that courtroom the day of the trial?

43. In your opinion, are you surprised by the tone and content of Commissioner Brooks' letter to District Attorney Lambertson?

44. What was the purpose behind the testimony of the first witness?

45. How did the second witness depict the physical condition of the Poncas when he arrested them?

46. Why was the Judge's reply to Lambertson's objection to allowing Standing Bear to testify important to the outcome of this trial?

47. Why do you think Standing Bear became so upset on the witness stand, such that the Judge had to calm him down?

48. Why do you think Lambertson did not call any government witnesses?

Chapter Fourteen

49. Why was this case called a case of "firsts"?

50. When did Lambertson know this was not an "open and shut case?"

51. Describe one key point that each lawyer made in the closing arguments that impressed you:

    Webster:

    Lambertson:

    Poppleton:

52. In your opinion, who was the most persuasive speaker that day?

53. Why do you think Poppleton was considered the preeminent trial lawyer of his day?

Chapter Fifteen

54. If you had been in the courtroom all day listening to the lawyers give their closing arguments and then heard Judge Dundy motion for Standing Bear to speak, how would you react?

55. Why was Bright Eyes so important to this moment, and what degree of confidence would she provide for Standing Bear?

56. Why was the opportunity to speak in the courtroom so important for Standing Bear's "quest for freedom?"

57. What gestures did Standing Bear employ in his speech and how important were they in conveying the emotions that must have been stirring in his heart?

58. How would you have reacted to Standing Bear's statement that "I am a Man" especially in light of Poppleton's closing argument?

59. In your opinion was Thomas Tibbles right or wrong in not publishing Standing Bear's metaphor in his newspaper article on the next day?

60. What does Standing Bear's speech add to your appreciation for this man?

Chapter Sixteen

61. If you had been in attendance during the two-day trial and were asked during the week of waiting for the judge to hand down his ruling, what would you tell your family, friends or co-workers what it was like to witness it all?

62. Describe what emotions the lawyers must have been feeling during the week of waiting.

63. In your opinion what do you think would have been the most difficult task Webster and Poppleton faced in preparing for such an unprecedented case?

64. Discuss what was at stake for Standing Bear, the Ponca prisoners, all Native Americans, and our Nation itself as everyone awaited the judge's decision.

Chapter Seventeen

65. Do Judge Dundy's opening remarks convey the emotions and struggle he faced and why he took a full ten days to rule in the case?

66. Discuss how Judge Dundy approached the issue of jurisdiction and what his ruling meant forty-eight years after Justice Marshall had ruled Native Americans were "wards of the government"?

67. What must Standing Bear have felt when he was told by his interpreter, most likely Bright Eyes, that a federal court judge had inserted into his decision Standing Bear's own words made on the witness stand that all he wanted "was to live and die in peace and be buried with his fathers?"

68. What role did the 14th Amendment have in Judge Dundy's ruling on the two issues in the case?

69. What do you think and feel when you read Judge Dandy's ruling?

Chapter Eighteen

70. Why would the government drop its appeal before it reached the Supreme Court?

71. How disappointed was Standing Bear when his initial efforts to bury the bones of his son Bear Shield failed?

72. What is revealed about the character of Standing Bear when shortly after his disappointment in not being able to bury his son, his thoughts and actions turn to thanking the newspaper reporter and his two lawyers?

73. Describe the symbolism of the gifts Standing Bear made to these three men and the words he spoke to them.

74. When anyone endures such great suffering as Standing Bear and his wife and friends did over nearly a year, what must they have felt when they were finally able to lay to rest Bear Shield on Ponca ancestral land?

75. What importance did the Eastern Tour have for the reform movement?

76. What was the impact of the Ponca Commission Report and the Senate Select Committee Report on the Poncas?

Chapter Nineteen

77. Describe the impact of the Standing Bear decision in later court cases.

Chapter Twenty

78. List the names of two or three of the people you think had the greatest impact on the outcome of this case, and give your reasons why you chose them.

79. Suggest ways diversity among the Omaha connection was important to the outcome of Standing Bear's quest for freedom.

80. What issues today could be solved if people from diverse backgrounds came together like these Omaha people did nearly a century and a half ago?

Chapter Twenty-One

81. Standing Bear won his quest for freedom. What does this mean?

Chapter Discussion Questions

Acknowledgements

I am grateful for the kindness of so many people who have assisted me in researching and writing this book. Betty Davis introduced me at the 130th anniversary celebration of the Trial of Standing Bear in May 2009 to two people who provided invaluable insights: the late Harold Anderson, former editor of the Omaha World Herald who shared his knowledge about General Crook and Fort Omaha; and Joe Starita who had just published his widely acclaimed book on Standing Bear, *I Am A Man*. Thank you Joe for raising the profile of Standing Bear for our nation.

A very special thank you to Judi gaiashkibos, Executive Director of the Nebraska Commission on Indian Affairs, and a Ponca herself, who gave me an extensive interview of all things Standing Bear. Judi is the granddaughter of Otto B. Knudsen, the last chief of the Ponca Tribe. In the immediate years before Standing Bear's death, Otto Knudsen's allotment of land made him a next-door neighbor to Standing Bear. Thank you, Judi, for allowing me to use the allotment township map in Chapter 18, and for sharing stories of your family and the rich history of the Poncas. A special thank you Judi for all you have done to honor Standing Bear with his statue in the U.S. Capitol and everything else you continue to promote that helps all Americans appreciate this heroic man.

Ten years after I spoke at the 130th Anniversary of the Trial of Standing Bear, Kathy Aultz, current Executive Director of the Douglas County Historical Society, graciously invited me to give another lecture on the grounds of Fort Omaha to commemorate the 140th Anniversary of the trial. A dinner followed my lecture in the Crook House. It was a memorable evening for me coming full circle from where it all began. Thank you, Kathy. And thank you Roxanne Knutson for coordinating the event.

Photos are a valuable component of any historical work so, I want to give special thanks to Ana Somers, Bill Gonzalez and Martha Miller.

Ana Somers, research specialist at the Douglas County Historical Society, gave generous time and effort to answer my many requests for the great photos of General Crook and his staff. Thanks Ana.

Bill Gonzalez, photo archivist at the Durham Museum which houses the unbelievable collection of mid 18th to early 19th century photos in the Bostwick-Frohardt Collection, is a treasure-trove of knowledge about everything concerning Omaha's early history. Special thanks Bill for your efforts to locate the pictures of Omaha showing the UPRR yards in the year my family emigrated from Ireland to work at that location; very meaningful for my Dwyer family.

Martha Vestecka Miller of the History Nebraska reference department provided most of the photos of Standing Bear, his family and home, as well as many of the participants in this story. Thank you, Martha, for your patience as I searched for just the right pictures to include. Thank you also Dell Darling of History Nebraska.

I am deeply honored that I was able to interview two distinguished members of the judiciary. The Honorable Thomas K. Harmon, Judge of the Douglas County Court always made himself available to answer my questions and made valuable suggestions for further research. I am especially grateful for the time given me by Chief Judge Laurie Smith Camp, of the United States District Court for Nebraska, one of the most knowledgeable persons on all matters concerning the trial. Her knowledge of the structure of the federal court system at the time of the trial, as well as her responses to my questions concerning why Judge Dundy may not have addressed certain issues in his ruling were precise and to the point. Thank you, Judge Harmon and Judge Smith Camp.

Along the way in researching this book I developed a friendship with Charles E. Wright. I was introduced to Charlie by way of Scott W. Shafer of the Nebraska Commission on Indian Affairs who felt we would have a lot in common to discuss (thanks Scott). Charles Wright is a retired attorney with the law firm of Cline, Williams, Wright, Johnson and Oldfather in Lincoln, Nebraska. The photo of Genio Lambertson sitting in his office is courtesy of Charlie. Lambertson was a member of a law firm that preceded Cline Williams. Charlie is the author of the book *Law At Little Big Horn* looking into the denial of due process to Native Americans. Charlie has been a tremendous source of knowledge on the legal issues involved in this case and I am eternally grateful for his wisdom. He and his wife Suzi established a scholarship at the University of Nebraska School of Law to benefit Native American students in pursuit of a law career. Thank you, Charlie, for the countless hours we have spent together on this project. You are a great blessing to me and all who know you.

Many thanks to Lisa K. Headley, proof-reader extraordinaire, and her husband Charles Jan Headley, my former law partner, for their support and feedback. They have been with me from the beginning. What else would I expect from such close friends of over 30 years.

In July 2018, I received a call from my good friend Bruce Haney, retired financial advisor, community activist, and lifelong supporter of all people and things that add to the beauty and culture of our society. Bruce invited me to give a lecture for the New Cassel Foundation on my book, so that he could have it professionally recorded before a live audience. In order to prepare for this lecture, I realized I needed to "finish" my research of primary sources (such research never really ends) and begin the actual writing of my book. Bruce and his wife Marlene are two of our dearest friends. They have always been willing to listen and encourage me in this project. Writing a book such as this and maintaining a law practice at the same time has been a challenge. But it has been made easier by their support. As a proud member of the "Haney's Staff Club" I can only say from the bottom of my heart, thank you Bruce for everything you have done for me.

I also want to thank Cindy Patach, Executive Director of the New Cassel Foundation, who hosted the lecture in November 2018. It was a beautiful event. By the way, it was Cindy's advertisement in the Omaha World Herald of the lecture that was seen by Scott W. Shafer in Lincoln, who "connected" me with Charles W. Wright.

Thank you, Jillian McClenahan, Anastasia Co., for your graphic design work on the cover that so beautifully depicts Standing Bear, and for deciphering my scribbles on the "Journey of Sorrows Map."

Thank you, Phil and Beth Black of *The Bookworm*, an independently owned bookstore in Omaha, for kindly reading my manuscript and offering helpful suggestions especially concerning all things that go into publishing and marketing a book in this digital age.

Thank you, Teresa A. Trumbly Lamsam, Associate Professor Emeritus in the School of Communication, University of Nebraska-Omaha, and a member of the Osage Tribe, for reading portions of my manuscript and for your very helpful comments.

Thank you, Kathy Kanavy, for praying for "a flow."

Thank you, Zachary Tilts, for ten years of reminding me "is it done yet?" Yes, Zach, it's done.

Thank you, Shelby S. Stevens, for your digital photography skills.

Special thanks to Jonathan Nitcher, Interlibrary Loan Coordinator, Criss Library, University of Nebraska-Omaha for hours spent locating Omaha newspapers for the time period of this book.

Thanks to my brother Thomas Dwyer for discovering in the basement of our family home, a pristine edition of *Wolfe's City Directory* for the years 1878-79.

Thanks to my office mates for listening to me every day talk about this book and still show interest: John Kellogg, Jeffrey Palzer, Julia Palzer, Rachael Kraft and Pamela Bissell.

Thanks also to all the civic organizations and clubs who have invited me these past ten years to share Standing Bear's story with their groups throughout Iowa and Nebraska. I have been honored to share him with all of you.

Special thanks to four students of the Creighton University School of Law who clerked in our office and researched cases and treaties pertinent to this book: Bryan Carter, Tonya Whipple, Seth Moen and Tom Schumacher. I am proud to say that today they are all distinguished practicing members of the Bar.

Thanks to Dr. Warren Francke, Professor Emeritus, University of Nebraska, Omaha, for his editing advice.

My very special thanks go to my friend of over 40 years, John P. Mullen, a Fellow of the American Trial Attorneys Association. John has read through my manuscript and its many revisions countless times and critiqued it with a "fine-tooth pen." I am grateful for his efforts in moving me away from the use of passive language (a lawyer's curse) to active shorter sentences. John's thoughtful questions led me to more research which has made this a better book than it would have been otherwise. His comments such as "judges sitting in Bench Trials issue rulings, juries issue verdicts," have helped me increase the accuracy of trial terminology. Thanks John, I could not have done this book without your help!

I have been blessed these past ten years with the support and encouragement of many people, but no one more crucial to the completion of this book than my wife of 35 years, Karen Kangas Dwyer Ph.D. Professor, School of Communications, University of Nebraska- Omaha. In the midst of writing her own books, giving lectures, and mentoring graduate students, Karen found time to listen to my new findings, read drafts, and edit and re-edit overly long sentences. In addition to her unparalleled media publishing skills, Karen is an award-winning professor and made major contributions to the book club discussion questions. Above all, she has been moved by the injustice done to Standing Bear and the Poncas, marveled at his eloquence, and urged me to finish this important story so that all can appreciate this great man and what he did for our country. I am grateful Karen that you walked this journey with me. All my love!

References

A Report of the Committee on The Judiciary. U.S. Senate, 41st Cong. 3rd Sess. 1870. no. 268.Washington: Government Printing Office.

Abbott, Charles Greeley, Editor. 1929,1944. *Smithsonian Series. Vol 4.* New York: Smithsonian Institution, 1944 (originally published in 1929)

American Heritage. 2017. *Standing Bear Goes to Court.* vol 62, Is. 3 (Summer).

Anderson, Grant K. 1977. *The Black Hills Exclusion Policy: Judicial Challenge.* Lincoln: Nebraska History *vol* 58, no 1 (Spring).

Annual Report of the Secretary of the Interior for 1877, Washington: Government Printing Office, 1877.

Annual Report of the Secretary of the Interior for 1878, Washington: Government Printing Office, 1878.

Annual Report of the Secretary of the Interior for 1879, Washington: Government Printing Office, 1879.

Appeal of Leah Brunt, Administratix, Estate of Theodore S. Brunt, United States Board of Tax Appeals, 5 B.T.A. (1926).

Bismark Tribune, August 12, 1874.

Blackstone, William. 1897. *Commentaries on The Laws of England. (1750).* Ed. W.M. Hardcastle Browne. St. Paul: West Publishing Company.

Black's Law Dictionary. 1990. Sixth Edition. St. Paul: West Publishing Company.

Bodayla, Stephen D. 1986. *Can an Indian Vote? Elk v. Wilkins. A Setback For Indian Citizenship.* Lincoln: Nebraska History vol 67, no 4 (Winter).

Boughter, Judith A. 1998. *BetrayingTthe Omaha Nation 1790-1916.* Norman: University of Oklahoma Press.

Bourke, John G. 2007. *Diaries. Vol. Three, June 1, 1875-June 22, 1880.* Ed. Charles M. Robinson III. Denton, TX: University of North Texas Press.

Bourke, John G. 2009. *Diaries. Vol. Four, July 3, 1880-May 22, 1881.* Ed. Charles M. Robinson III. Denton, TX: University of North Texas Press.

Bourke, John G. 1971. *On the Border With Crook.* Lincoln: University of Nebraska Press.

Brown, Wallace. 1969. *George L. Miller and The Boosting of Omaha.* Nebraska History 50, 277-291 (Fall).

Capps, Benjamin. 1973. *The Old West: The Indians.* New York: Time-Life Books.

Carlson, Paul H. 1998. *The Plains Indians.* College Station: Texas A&M University Press.

Cases Determined in the United States, Circuit Courts for the Eighth Circuit, Vol. 5. Reported by John F. Dillon, the Circuit Judge. Davenport, Iowa: Egbert, Fidlar & Chambers, 1880.

Catlin, George. 1973. *Letters and Notes on The Manners, Customs and Conditions of North American Indians. Vol. 1.* New York: Dover Publications.

Cherokee Nation v. The State of Georgia. 30 U.S.1. (1831).

Cohen, Felix S. *1971. Felix S. Cohen's Handbook of Federal Indian Law.* Albuquerque: University of New Mexico Press.

Dana Leigh Thompson v. County of Franklin et.al, 2001 WL 34355597. N.D.-NY. (2001).

Dando-Collins, Stephen. 2004. *Standing Bear Is A Person.* Cambridge, MA: DaCapo Press.

Danzinger, Danny and John Gillingham. 2005. *1215 The Year of Magna Carta.* New York: Simon & Schuster-Touchstone.

DeMaillie, Raymond J. 1984. 'The Buffalo' in The First Voices. Nebraskaland Mag. *Vol.* 62. no 1. Lincoln: Nebraska Games and Park Commission.

deTocqueville, Alexis. 1835. 1956. Democracy In America. Originally published in 1835. /Edited by Richard D. Heffner. New York: The New American Library, 1956.

Department of the Interior, Office of Indian Affairs. 1879. Letter of E.A. Brooks, Acting Commissioner to G.M. Lambertson U.S. District Attorney, April 22, 1879 (Ponca, L. 358, 1879).

Dorsey, Rev. James Owen. 1886. *Migrations of Siouan Tribes.* The American Naturalist *Vol.* XX-no. 30 (March).

Douglas County Historical Society. 2008. *The Banner.* Omaha (December).

Dred Scott v. Sandford, 60 U.S. 393, (1856)

Elk v. Wilkins, 112 U.S. 94 (1884).

Ex parte Merryman. 17 F. Cas.144. Md. (1861).

Fletcher, Alice C. and Francis LaFlesche. 1911. 1992. *The Omaha Tribe Vol. I.* Lincoln: University of Nebraska Press, 1992. (originally published by Smithsonian Institution Bureau of American Ethnology. Washington D.C.: Government Printing Office, 1911).

Fletcher, Alice C. and Francis LaFlesche. 1911. 1992. *The Omaha Tribe Vol. II.* Lincoln: University of Nebraska Press, 1992. (originally published by Smithsonian Institution Bureau of American Ethnology. Washington D.C.: Government Printing Office, 1911).

Fort Omaha Walking Tour Guide. Omaha: Metropolitan Community College.

General Crook House Museum Tour Guide. 2018. Douglas County Historical Society Omaha.

Green, Norma Kidd. 1969. *Iron Eye's Family. The Children of Joseph LaFlesche.* Lincoln: Nebraska State Historical Society.

Hayt, E.A. 1877. *Journal of March.* The Annual Report given by E.A. Hayt, Commissioner for Indian Affairs, to the Secretary of the Interior for the year 1877.

Howard, James H. 1965. 1995. *The Ponca Tribe.* Lincoln: University of Nebraska Press, 1995. (originally published by the Smithsonian Institution Bureau of American Ethnology Bulletin no. 195. Washington: Government Printing Office, 1965).

In the Matter of the Adoption of C.D.K., a Minor Child, 2009 WL 2494618 (D.UT 2009)

Jackson, Helen Hunt. 1885. 2015. *A Century of Dishonor: A Sketch of The United States Government's Dealings With Some Of The Indian Tribes.* The Project Gutenberg 2015 (www.guttenberg.org) (originally published in Boston: 1885).

James E. O'Neill v. Eldon Morse, 20 Mich. App. 679, 174 N.W.2nd 575, (1969).

Johnson and Graham's Lessee v. William M'Intosh. 21 U.S. 543. (1823).

King, James. 1969. *A Better Way: General George Crook and the Ponca Indians.* Lincoln: Nebraska History *Vol.* 50 (Fall).

Lake, James A. Sr. 1981. *Standing Bear! Who?* Nebraska Law Review *Vol.* 60, *No.* 3: 451-503.

Lambertson, Genio M. *Indian Citizenship.* 1886. 20 ALR 183.

Larsen, Lawrence H. and Barbara J. Cottrell. 1997. *The Gate City: A History of Omaha.* Lincoln: University of Nebraska Press.

Mathes, Valerie Sherer and Richard Lowitt. 2003. *The Standing Bear Controversy: Prelude To Indian Reform.* Chicago: University of Illinois Press.

Mathes, Valerie Sherer, Editor. 1998. *The Indian Reform Letters of Helen Hunt Jackson, 1879-1885. Norman:* University of Oklahoma Press.

McGinty, Brian. 2008. *Lincoln and The Courts.* Cambridge, MA: Harvard University Press.

Moulton, Gary E. Editor. 1987. *The Definitive Journals of Lewis & Clark Vol. 3 of the Nebraska Edition.* Lincoln: University of Nebraska Press.

Nichols, Roger L. 1965. *General Henry Atkinson.* Norman: University of Oklahoma Press.

Olson, James C. 1974. *History of Nebraska.* Lincoln: University of Nebraska Press.

Omaha Daily Bee. December 4, 1880.

Omaha Herald. April 1, 1879.

Omaha Herald. May 2, 1879.

Omaha Herald. May 3, 1879.

Omaha Herald. May 4, 1879.

Omaha Herald. May 6, 1879.

Omaha Herald. May 7, 1879.
Omaha Herald. May 13, 1879.

Omaha Herald. May 15, 1879.

Omaha Herald. May 18, 1879.

Omaha Herald. May 20, 1879.

Omaha Republican. May 4, 1879.

Omaha Sun, August 7, 1975.

Omaha Times. February 10, 1859.

Omaha World Herald, December 3, 2013.

Peter L. Poodry v. Tonawanda Band of Seneca Indians, 85 F.3rd 874 (Ind. 1996).

Ponca Tribe of Indians v. Makh-pi-ah-lu-tah, or Red Cloud, in his own behalf and in behalf of the Sioux Tribe of Indians. Fed. Dist. Ct. (NE: 1880).

Poppleton, Andrew J. 1915. *Reminiscences.* Lincoln: History Nebraska.

Poppleton, Caroline L. 1915. *The War Bonnet.* Lincoln: History Nebraska.

Prucha, Francis Paul. 1996. *The Great Father.* Lincoln: University of Nebraska Press.

Reilly, Hugh J. 2011. *Bound to Have Blood. Frontier Newspapers and The Plains Indian Wars.* Lincoln: University of Nebraska Press.

Reply of the Boston Committee to Secretary of Interior Carl Schurz. Boston: Frank Wood Printer, 1881.

Report of the Board of Indian Commissioners. 1885. H.R. Exec. Doc.No.1, 49th Cong.1st Sess.

Russell Means v. Navajo Nation and United States of America, 432 F.3rd 924 (CA 2005)

Schach, Paul. 1994. *Maximilian, Prince of Wied (1782-1867): Reconsidered.* Lincoln: Great Plains Quarterly, 853, http//digitalcommons.unl.edu./greatplainsquarterly/853.

Schurr, Nancy. 2017. *Cherokee Removal & The Trail of Tears.* Retrieved from the Digital Public Library of America, https://dp/la/primary-source-sets-cherokee-removal-the-trail-of-tears.

Senate Select Committee Report Concerning the Removal and Situation of the Ponca Indians. *No.* 670, The U.S. Senate, 46th Cong. 2nd Sess. 1880.

Sheldon, Addison, E. 1926. *History and Stories of Nebraska.* Lincoln: The University Publishing Co.

Slaughter House Cases. 83 U.S. (16 Wall.) 36 (1873).

Starita, Joe. 2009. *I Am A Man.* New York: St. Martin's Press.

State v. Central Lumber Co. 123 NW 504 (SD 1909)

State Ex. Rel. Bancroft v. Frear, Secretary of State, 144 Wis.79, 128 N.W. 1068 (1910).

The General Allotment Act. 1887. *24 Stat.388. Ch 119, 25 USCA 331. https:*//www.ourdocuments.gov/doc.php?doc=50&Page=Transcript.

The Habeas Corpus Act. 1679. English Statute of 31 Car. II, C.2.

The Habeas Corpus Act. *1871.* 14 Stat. 385. Codified in Title 28 of the U.S.C.A.legisworks.org/sa/14/stats/STATUTE-14-Pg385.pdf.

The Homestead Act. 1862. https://www.archives.gov/education/lessons/homestead-act

The Indian Appropriation Act. 1871. 16 Stat. 566.

The Indian Freedom Citizenship Suffrage Act. *1924.* 8 U.S.C. Ch 12, subch 111, 104 1b. https://legislink.org/us/stat.

The Indian Removal Act. 1830.

The Judiciary Act. 1789. 1 Stat.73 (Codified in Title 28 of the U.S.C.A.).

The Kansas-Nebraska Act. 1854. 10 Stat. 277. https://legislink.org/us/stat.

The Ordinance for The Government of The Territory of United States Northwest of The River Ohio. https://www.ourdocuments.gov/doc.php?flash=false&doc=8 &page=Transcript.

The Ponca Relief Bill. 1881. 21 Stat. 422.

The Ponca Restoration Act. 1990. Pub L.No.101-484. 5,104 Stat.1167. as amended.

Tibbles, Thomas H. (1880) 1972. *The Ponca Chiefs*. Lincoln: University of Nebraska Press.

Tibbles, Thomas H. 1969. *Buckskin and Blanket Days*. Lincoln: University of Nebraska Press.

Tibbles, Thomas H. Thomas Tibbles Papers. Smithsonian Institution http://collections.si.edu/search/detail/ead_collection:sova-nmai-ac-066.

Treaty with The Poncas 1817. http://www.firstpeople.us/FP-Html-Treaties/Treaties.html.

Treaty with The Poncas 1825. http://www.firstpeople.us/FP-Html-Treaties/Treaties.html.

Treaty with The Poncas 1858. http://www.firstpeople.us/FP-Html-Treaties/Treaties.html.

Treaty with The Poncas 1865. http://www.firstpeople.us/FP-Html-Treaties/Treaties.html.

Treaty with The Sioux Brule 1868. http://www.firstpeople.us/FP-Html-Treaties/Treaties.html.

*United States Constitution. 1*990. Black's Law Dictionary. Sixth Edition. St. Paul: West Publishing Company. (1639-1650).

United States v. Schooner Peggy. 5 U.S. 103,109-110, 2L.Ed.49.51. (1801)

United States ex rel. Standing Bear v. Crook 5 Dil. 453, 25 F. Cas. 695 D. Nebraska (1879).

U.S. Senate. 46th Cong. 3rd Sess. (1881). *A Report of The Commission Appointed December 18, 1880, to Ascertain the Facts In Regard To The Removal of the Ponca Indians.* (The Ponca Commission) Select Comm. Ex. Doc. No. 30.

U.S. Senate, 47th Cong. 1st Sess. 1881. Report of the Secretary of the Interior. H.R. Ex. Doc. No.1.

United States Office of the Federal Register & Congressional Quarterly's Guide to U.S. Elections. 4th edition. (2001)

Utley, Robert M. 1984. *The Indian Frontier of the American West 1846-1890.* Albuquerque: University of New Mexico Press.

Webster, John and Andrew Poppleton. 1880. *Report To The Omaha Ponca Indian Committee.*

Wilson, Dorothy. 1974. *Bright Eyes.* New York: McGraw-Hill.

Wilson, Ray D. 1983. *Nebraska Historical Tour Guide.* Carpentersville, IL: Crossroads Communication.

Wishart, David J. 1994. *An Unspeakable Sadness: The Dispossession of The Nebraska Indians* Lincoln: University of Nebraska Press.

Wishart, David J., Editor 2007. *Encyclopedia of The Great Plains Indians.* Lincoln: University of Nebraska Press.

Wolfe, J.M. 1878. *Omaha City Directory 1878-79.* Omaha: Herald Publishing House.

Worcester, Donald E. 1975. "*The Friends of The Indian and The Peace Policy'* in *Forked Tongues and Broken Treaties.* Editor Donald E. Worcester. Caldwell, ID: Caxton Printers.

Wright, Charles E. 2016. *Law at Little Big Horn.* Lubbock: Texas Tech University Press.

Writ of Habeas Corpus, Douglas County Historical Society.

Wunder, John R. and Mark R. Scherer. 2019. *Echo of Its Time: The History of the Federal District Court of Nebraska, 1867-1933.* Lincoln: University of Nebraska Press.

Endnotes

[1] For more information on the "Indian Territory," see Dianna Everett, "Indian Territory," *The Encyclopedia of Oklahoma History and Culture*, https://www.okhistory.org/publications/enc/entry.php?entry=IN018.

[2] O. H. April 13, 1879.

[3] Tibbles *Buckskin*, 193.

[4] Bourke, *vol.* 3, 180.

[5] O.H. May 2, 1879.

[6] Howard, J., 14.

[7] Dorsey, 215.

[8] Fletcher, *vol.* 1, 35.

[9] Hartley Burr Alexander (1873-1939) was inducted into the Nebraska Hall of Fame in 1984. The inscription on his bust states that he as a "philosopher, poet and teacher; an interpreter of Native American Culture; and thematic consultant for the Nebraska capitol and other nationally prominent structures."

[10] Dorsey, 215.

[11] Dorsey, 215; Howard, J., 15.

[12] Dorsey, 215; Howard, J., 15.

[13] Nebraska was admitted to the Union on March 1, 1867. South Dakota and North Dakota were admitted to the Union on November 2, 1889.

[14] Dorsey, 219.

[15] Ibid.

[16] DeMallie, 61.

[17] *Note:* Capps reports for example that the horns of the buffalo were used to make rings, spoons, cups, ladles, and quills; and the bones of the buffalo were used to make arrowheads, sewing awls, hide scrappers and knives, 74-75.

[18] Howard, 19.

[19] Howard, 8.

[20] Fletcher, *vol.* 1, 95-990.

[21] Ibid.

[22] Moulton, 399-400.

[23] Catlin, ix.

[24] Catlin, 212-213.

[25] Schach, 12-13.

[26] Carlson, 12.

[27] Moulton, 399-400.

[28] *State v. Central Lumber Co.* 123 NW 504, (SD 1909).

[29] Howard, J., 16.

[30] Howard, J., 19.

[31] Ibid.

[32] Senate Select Committee Report, Testimony of Standing Bear, 17.

[33] Fletcher *vol.* 1, 269.

[34] Howard, J. 91; Fletcher *vol.* 1, 208-209.

[35] Howard J. 94; Fletcher *vol.* 1, 47-48.

[36] Fletcher *vol.* 1, 213.

[37] Howard, J., 96

[38] Ibid.

[39] Fletcher *vol.* 1, 215.

[40] Howard, J., 95.

[41] Ibid.

[42] Johnson, parg. 11-12.

[43] Johnson, parg. 19. *Note:* A good discussion of this case can be found in *Buying Land from the Indians* by Blake A. Watson, University of Oklahoma Press, 2012.

[44] Cherokee, parg.13.

[45] *Note:* Even though the Declaration of Independence is not part of the law, it certainly was a source of inspiration to Abraham Lincoln in his Gettysburg Address, and as a guide for the framers of the Fourteenth Amendment.

[46] Prucha, 111.

[47] Utley, 41-43; Wishart, 55.

[48] Indian Removal Act of 1830. (See Endnote #1 for description of "Indian Territory.")

[49] Kansas-Nebraska Act of 1854.

[50] Homestead Act of 1862.

[51] Ordinance Sec 14. *Art* 3.

[52] Wright, 66.

[53] Black's Law Dictionary, 1645.

[54] Black's Law Dictionary, 1643.

[55] Black's Law Dictionary, 1641.

[56] Ibid.

[57] Court in *United States v. Schooner Peggy* 5 U.S. 103, 109-110, 2 L. Ed. 49, 51 (1801).

[58] Treaty with the Poncas 1817. *Note:* This is the same William Clark who had entered the Ponca village in 1804 on the Lewis & Clark Expedition. Chouteau was a member of the famous St. Louis family who controlled much of the trading with the Great Plains tribes for many years.

[59] Nichols, 97-98.

[60] Treaty with the Poncas, 1825, *Art.* 3.

[61] Wishart, *Unspeakable Sadness,* 27, 133.

[62] Carlson, 8; Wishart, *Encyclopedia*, 184-185.

[63] Treaty with the Poncas 1858, *Art* 2.

[64] Treaty with the Poncas, 1858, *Art* 1.

[65] Report of Commissioner for Indian Affairs, 1858.

[66] Wishart, *Unspeakable Sadness,* 135.

[67] Treaty with the Poncas 1865, *Art* 2.

[68] Ibid.

[69] Treaty with the Sioux Brule 1868, *Art* 2.

[70] Sheldon, 223.

[71] Senate Select Committee Report, V.

[72] Indian App. Act 1871.

[73] Senate Select Committee Report, II.

[74] *Note:* Rev. William H. Hare, Bishop of the Episcopal Church, who for many years ministered in the Ponca Village as well as other villages, confirmed this in testimony before a Senate Select Committee in 1880: "The Indians have no representatives who are competent to act for them…interpreters are too often very unreliable; and what they say with their mouth is often very different from what is written on the paper." (Senate Select Committee on Ponca Removal, February 16, 1880, 117).

[75] Prucha, 180.

[76] Ibid.

[77] Prucha, 174.

[78] Fletcher, *vol* I, 290-311.

[79] Fletcher, *vol* II, 635.

[80] *Note:* A Senate Select Committee on the Ponca Removal of 1880 (p. 382-395) provided numerous letters and reports from government officials verifying the constant Brule attacks on the Poncas during the 1870's.

[81] Senate Select Committee Report, 122-123.

[82] Bismark, 1.

[83] Anderson, 1. (*Note:* There was a provision in the Fort Laramie Treaty that excluded anyone from trespassing on these Sioux lands. To avoid a battle with the Sioux, the government arrested a trespasser named John Gordon, the leader of a group of gold-seeking miners. Gordon's attorney filed a Writ of Habeas Corpus which was heard in the federal courthouse in Omaha before Judge Elmer S. Dundy in the summer of 1875. For more details on this case, see *The Black Hills Exclusion Policy* by Anderson.)

[84] Wright, 82-89.

[85] Wright, 233.

[86] Bourke, On the Border, 232.

[87] Senate Select Committee, Report, Testimony of Kemble, 49-50.

[88] Senate Select Committee Report, Testimony of Standing Bear, 3.

[89] Senate Select Committee Report, Testimony of Standing Bear, 4.

[90] Senate Select Committee Report, Testimony of Standing Bear, 13.

[91] Senate Select Committee Report, Testimony of Standing Bear, 5.

[92] Senate Select Committee Report, Testimony of Kemble, 52.

[93] Senate Select Committee Report, Testimony of Standing Bear, 18.

[94] Ponca Commission Report, 14.

[95] Ibid.

[96] Jackson, Century, Project Gutenberg Ch VI; Senate Select Committee Report, Testimony of Standing Bear, 6-7.

[97] Senate Select Committee Report, Testimony of Bright Eyes, 22.

[98] Senate Select Committee Report, Testimony of Bright Eyes, 23.

[99] Senate Select Committee Report, 432.

[100] Senate Select Committee Report, 23.

[101] Senate Select Committee Report, 22.

[102] Jackson, Century, Project Gutenberg Ch. VI.

[103] Senate Select Committee Report, VII.

[104] Senate Select Committee Report, VIII.

[105] Hayt, E. A., Annual Report given by the Commissioner for Indian Affairs to the Secretary of the Interior for 1877(includes Journal of the March by Inspector E. A. Howard).

[106] Fletcher *vol.* 1, 51.

[107] Hayt, E. A., 1877.

[108] Tibbles, *Ponca Chiefs*, 13; also see Standing Bear's testimony before the Senate Select Committee Report, 1.

[109] Senate Select Committee Report, Testimony of Tibbles, 41.

[110] Senate Select Committee Report, Testimony of White Eagle, 78.

[111] Senate Select Committee Report, Testimony of White Eagle, 15.

[112] Hayt, E. A., 1877, 97-99.

[113] Omaha World Herald December 3, 2013.

[114] Senate Select Committee Report, Testimony of Bright Eyes, 24; Green, 57.

[115] Hayt, E. A., 1877, 97.

[116] Hayt, E. A., 1877, 100.

[117] Hayt, E. A., 1877, 101.

[118] Senate Select Committee Report, Testimony of Standing Bear, 12, 20.

[119] Senate Select Committee Report, XIV.

[120] Hayt, E. A., 1877.

[121] O.H. April 1, 1879; and Senate Select Committee Report, Testimony of Standing Bear, 10.

[122] Ponca Commission, 16.

[123] Senate Select Committee Report, Testimony of White Eagle, 211.

[124] Senate Select Committee Report, VIII.

[125] Cherokee, parg. 13.

[126] Howard, 93.

[127] Tibbles, *Ponca Chiefs*, 15.

[128] Tibbles, *Ponca Chiefs*, 15; and Senate Select Committee Report, Testimony of Standing Bear, 16.

[129] Tibbles, *Ponca Chiefs*, 16.

[130] Ibid, 43.

[131] Ibid, 16.

[132] Senate Select Committee Report, Testimony of Bright Eyes, 29.

[133] Until the Fall of 1879, George and Mary Crook lived at 596 18th Street in downtown Omaha. *Wolfe's City Directory*, 121.

[134] General Dodge House Tour Guide; Wilson, 20-22.

[135] For more information, see www.Douglas County History.org.

[136] General Dodge House Tour Guide; Wolfe. 73; Fort Omaha Tour Guide.

[137] Ibid.

[138] *Note:* According to the Crook House Data Printout, "General Crook disliked formality and social affairs and never wore his uniform when he could avoid it. His two great passions were hunting and fishing. He often left the Fort and went for days into the wilderness to hunt with his dogs. He also spent many hours pursuing his hobby of taxidermy, particularly the tanning of pelts, and was especially proud of a large grizzly bear rug. Mary Crook (nee Mary Tapscott Dailey) was born in Maryland and married George Crook on August 22, 1865. They had no children. Mary died in 1895 and is buried alongside her husband in Arlington National Cemetery."

[139] Fletcher *vol.* II, 635.

[140] Worcester, 280; For more details, see Worcester, 278-281.

[141] Tibbles, *Buckskin*, 187, 193. *Note:* Iron Eye, Chief of the Omaha Tribe, would be aware of the fact that General Crook and Thomas Tibbles had both been initiated into his tribe's secret society known as "The Soldier's Lodge" and therefore, he would have felt a common bond with both men. Because of this common bond, he knew Crook would not arrest him and his daughter Bright Eyes for leaving their reservation without government permission to visit him. Iron Eye also knew Crook would listen respectfully as they related the Poncas' story.

[142] Wolfe's City Director, 227.

[143] Tibbles, *Ponca Chiefs*, 18; Bourke, Diaries *vol.* 3, 492.

[144] *Wolfes City Directory*, 227.

[145] Tibbles, *Ponca Chiefs*,18-19; Tibbles, *Buckskin*, 193-196.

[146] *Note:* I have not discovered any direct written evidence of Iron Eye and Bright Eyes going to see General Crook that Sunday evening, or that they accompanied him on his midnight ride to see Thomas Tibbles. But it seems to me there is strong and credible circumstantial evidence that they did just that: **(1)** I concur with Stephen Dando-Collins's belief (*Standing Bear Is A Person*, 240) that there could be no other source for Crook's knowledge of the Ponca removal story of 1877 and Standing Bear's return in 1879 than Bright Eyes. However, I believe that her father Iron Eye was also a source of Crook's knowledge as both of them were eyewitnesses to both events as described in Bright Eyes testimony before the Senate Select Committee on the Ponca Removal in 1880 (p. 24, 29). Iron Eye more than likely would have accompanied Bright Eyes to see Crook because he would have been concerned for her safety traveling 100 miles from Decatur to Fort Omaha if

she went alone, in addition to the risk she could be arrested for leaving the reservation without government permission. Iron Eye likely believed Crook would treat the story with more credibility if he, Chief of the Omaha tribe, could verify the story along with Bright Eyes, since he knew of Crook's respect for Native Americans and because he knew that Tibbles and Crook were members of the Soldiers Lodge. **(2)** There is another reason why I believe Iron Eye and Bright Eyes accompanied General Crook to visit Tibbles at such a late hour. Crook would have no other reason to wait to see Tibbles at midnight unless he had Iron Eye and Bright Eyes with him so they would not be seen on the streets of Omaha during daylight hours where they could be arrested. Crook was still living at his home with his wife Mary at 596 18th Street in downtown Omaha until the fall of 1879, and not at Fort Omaha (*Wolfe's City Directory*, 121) so, he could have easily waited until morning to visit with Tibbles if he didn't have Iron Eye and Bright Eyes with him.

[147] Tibbles, *Ponca Chiefs*, 19, 27.

[148] *Omaha Herald* (O.H), April 1, 1879.

[149] O.H. April 1, 1879.

[150] Ibid.

[151] Ibid.

[152] Ibid.

[153] Ibid.

[154] Ibid.

[155] Ibid.

[156] Ibid.

[157] Ibid.

[158] Tibbles, *Ponca Chiefs*, 27.

[159] Tibbles, *Ponca Chiefs*, 28.

[160] Ibid.

[161] Bourke, Diaries *vol.* 3, 185.

[162] Bourke, Diaries *vol.* 3, 180.

[163] Ibid.

[164] Ibid.

[165] Bourke, Diaries *vol.* 3. 182.

[166] Bourke, Diaries *vol.* 3, 183.

[167] Bourke, Diaries *vol.* 3, 185.

[168] Ibid.

[169] Tibbles *Ponca Chiefs*, 32.

[170] Tibbles *Ponca Chiefs*, 33.

[171] O.H. April 1, 1879.

[172] Ibid.

[173] Wolfe, 296-297). *Note:* Larsen & Cottrell cite the rapid growth of Omaha's population: the 1860 census (1883), the 1870 census (16,083), and the 1900 census (103,000).

[174] Wolfe, 284; Omaha Sun, August 7, 1975.

[175] Tibbles, *Ponca Chiefs*, 34; Wolfe, 284.

[176] Wolfe, 237; Poppleton, Rem 9; Douglas County Historical Society Banner December 2008, 11.

[177] *Note:* As the first lawyer to open a law practice in Omaha, Poppleton also led the way in advertising his services. The following ad was placed in the February 10, 1859 edition of the Omaha Times: "Andrew J. Poppleton and George E. Lake, attorneys at law. Dealers in land warrants and exchanges, loan and collection agents, Omaha, Nebraska."

[178] Tibbles, *Ponca Chiefs*, 353; Wolfe 237.

[179] Poppleton. *Reminiscences,* 32.

[180] Black's Law Dictionary, 709.

[181] Poppleton. *Reminiscences,* 32.

[182] Tibbles, *Buckskin*, 199.

[183] Black's Law Dictionary, 1647.

[184] A Report of the Committee on the Judiciary, 1870, 10.

[185] Tibbles, *Ponca Chiefs*, 34-35.

[186] Danzinger & Gillingerham, *1215 The Year of Magna Carta*, 83.

[187] Blackstone, 437; The Habeas Corpus Act of 1679.

[188]Blackstone, 438.

[189] Black's Law Dictionary, 1642.

[190] Judiciary Act. Ch.XX. Sec.14 (1789).

[191] Habeas Corpus Act. Ch. XXVII and XXVIII (1867).

[192] McGinty, 69.

[193] *Ex parte Merryman*, 17 F. Cas.144. (Md.1861).

[194] Application for the Writ of Habeas Corpus, April 8, 1879, and the Return of General Crook, April 11, 1879, full text available in Tibbles, *Ponca Chiefs*, 36.

[195] Ibid, 36

[196] Ibid, 37.

[197] Ibid, 37.

[198] Ibid, 38.

[199] Ibid, 38-39.

[200] Tibbles, *Buckskin*, 199.

[201] Tibbles, *Ponca Chiefs*, 36.
[202] Federal Judicial Center; Wunder, p. 44.

[203] The Writ, Douglas County Historical Society, 6-7.

[204] Telegram from Carl Schurz to the U.S. Attorney General, April 9, 1879.

[205] Tibbles, *Ponca Chiefs*, 47-48.

[206] Tibbles, *Ponca Chiefs*, 49.

[207] Tibbles, *Ponca Chiefs*, 50, 52.

[208] *Note:* One year after the Standing Bear Trial, Lieutenant John G. Bourke made an entry in his diary for May 13, 1880 noting that a grand jury in New Jersey had indicted Commissioner Hayt for "falsely certifying to the financial status of a defunct savings bank of which he was president." (Bourke, Diaries *vol.* 3, 190).

[209] Interview on December 2, 2018 with Charles E. Wright, retired attorney with the Lincoln law firm of Cline Williams Wright Johnson & Oldfather. The law firm of Lambertson & Hall (1894-1902) was a predecessor to the Cline Williams Wright law firm.

[210] Bourke *vol.* 3. 187.

[211] O.H. May 2, 1879.

[212] *Wolfe's City Directory*, 35.

[213] *Wolfe's City Directory*, 307.

[214] Reilly, 97-110.

[215] *Note:* According to *Wolfe's City Directory*, Omaha was awash with newspapers. There were four daily/weekly English newspapers in Omaha at the time of the trial: **1)** *The Omaha Herald* (O.H.), founded in 1865, George L. Miller editor, located at 257 Farnam Street. At the time of the trial, the front page of this newspaper identified itself as the *Omaha Herald*; whereas, the editorial page of the paper identified itself as the Omaha Daily Herald. **2)** *The Omaha Bee,* founded in 1871, Edward Rosewater editor, located at 158 Farnam Street; **3**) *The Omaha Republican*, founded in 1858, D. C. Brooks editor, located at 220 Douglas Street; and **4)** *The Omaha Evening News*, J. C. Wheeler editor, located at 521 13th Street. Omaha also had three newspapers who published only once a month in English. In addition, there was one German weekly, one Bohemian weekly, and one Danish weekly (*Wolfe's City Directory*, 307). In 1885, Gilbert M. Hitchcock founded the *Omaha Evening World.* In 1889, he purchased the *Omaha Herald*, and the two papers merged into the *Omaha World Herald.*

[216] Brown, 277.

[217] *Wolfe's City Directory.*

[218] Tibbles, *Buckskin*, 200.

[219] O.H. May 2, 1879.

[220] Ibid.

[221] Ibid.

[222] Ibid.

[223] Department of the Interior, Office of Indian Affairs, Letter of E.A. Brooks, Acting Commissioner to G.M. Lambertson U.S. District Attorney, April 22, 1879 (Ponca, L. 358, 1879), 1.

[224] Ibid, 3.

[225] Ibid, 5.

[226] O.H. May 2, 1879.

[227] Ibid.

[228] O.H. May 2, 1879; Tibbles, *Ponca Chiefs*, 66-67.

[229] O.H. May 2, 1879.

[230] Tibbles, *Ponca Chiefs*, 68-69.

[231] Ibid.

[232] Tibbles, *Ponca Chiefs*, 69-70.

[233] Tibbles, *Ponca Chiefs*, 72.

[234] Tibbles, *Ponca Chiefs*, 73.

[235] Tibbles, *Ponca Chiefs*, 77.

[236] Tibbles, *Ponca Chiefs*, 78.

[237] Tibbles, *Ponca Chiefs*, 79.

[238] O.H. May 2, 1879.

[239] Ibid.

[240] *Cherokee* decision.

[241] O.H. May 2, 1879.

[242] Ibid.

[243] O.H. May 2, 1879.

[244] Ibid.

[245] Ibid.

[246] Tibbles, *Ponca Chiefs*, 79.

[247] Tibbles, *Ponca Chiefs*, 83.

[248] O.H. May 2, 1879.

[249] Ibid.

[250] Ibid.

[251] Tibbles, *Ponca Chiefs*, 90.

[252] O.H. May 2, 1879.

[253] Ibid.

[254] Tibbles, *Buckskin*, 200.

[255] Ibid.

[256] Cherokee Nation.

[257] O.H. May 2, 1879.

[258] O.H. May 2, 1879; O.H. May 3, 1879.

[259] O.H.-May 3, 1879.

[260] Ibid.

[261] Ibid.

[262] Ibid.

[263] Ibid.

[264] O.H. May 4.

[265] O.H. May 3, 1879; Poppleton. *Reminiscences,* 32.

[266] O.H. May 4, 1879.

[267] O.H. May 3, 1879.

[268] Ibid.'

[269] Ibid.

[270] O.H. May 4, 1879.

[271] O.H. May 3, 1879.

[272] Ibid.

[273] Ibid.

[274] Ibid.

[275] Ibid.

[276] A Report of the Committee on the Judiciary, 1870.

[277] O.H. May 3, 1879.

[278] Ibid.

[279] Ibid.

[280] *Dred Scott v. Sandford,* 60 U.S.393 (1856).

[281] O.H. May 7, 1879.

[282] Ibid.

[283] Cases Determined in the United States Circuit Court for the Eighth Circuit, *vol.* 5, 1880, 457.

[284] Ibid, 456.

[285] Ibid, 456.

[286] O.H. May 7, 1879.

[287] O.H. May 3, 1879.

[288] Poppleton. *Reminiscences,* 32.

[289] O.H. May 4, 1879.

[290] Ibid.

[291] Ibid.

[292] Ibid.

[293] Ibid.

[294] Ibid.

[295] Ibid.

[296] Ibid.

[297] Ibid.

[298] O.H. May 6, 1879.

[299] Ibid.

[300] Ibid.

[301] O.H. May 7, 1879.

[302] Ibid.

[303] O.H. May 3, 1879.

[304] Ibid.

[305] Sheldon, 229-230; Senate Select Committee Report, Testimony of Bright Eyes, February 13, 1880, 20-22.

[306] Tibbles, *Buckskin*, 200.

[307] O.H. May 3, 1879.

[308] Tibbles, *Buckskin*, 200.

[309] O.H. May 3, 1879.

[310] O.H. May 3, 1879.

[311] Tibbles, *Buckskin*, 201. *Note:* In addition, Caroline Poppleton related in her letter, *The War Bonnet,* that when Standing Bear came to her home on May 18, 1879 to thank her husband for representing him in the trial, Standing Bear said: "I believe I told you in the courtroom that God made me a man."

[312] Ibid. *Note:* Standing Bear spoke in a similar metaphor during his interview in General Crook's office on March 31, 1879 (*Bourke's Diary*, vol. 3, 183.

[313] O.H. May 4, 1879.

[314] Tibbles, *Buckskin*, 202,

[315] Bourke, Diaries *vol.* 3, 182-183.

[316] Poppleton. Caroline, 1915.

[317] Cases Determined in the United States Circuit Court for the Eighth Circuit, vol. 5, 461.

[318] de Tocquiville, 123.

[319] Poppleton. *Reminiscences,* 32.

[320] O.H. May 13, 1879.

[321] Cases Determined in the United States Circuit Court for the Eighth Circuit, *vol.* 5, 1880, 453-469.

[322] Ibid, 454.

[323] Ibid, 454.

[324] Ibid, 455.

[325] Ibid, 457.

[326] Ibid.

[327] Ibid, 458.

[328] Ibid.

[329] Ibid, 459.

[330] Ibid.

[331] Black's Law Dictionary, 1057.

[332] Cases Determined in the United States Circuit Court for the Eighth Circuit, *vol.* 5, 1880, 459.

[333] Ibid, 460.

[334] Ibid.

[335] Ibid, 461.

[336] Ibid, 462.

[337] Ibid, 463.

[338] Ibid.

[339] Ibid, 464.

[340] Ibid.

[341] Ibid.

[342] Ibid, 467.

[343] Ibid, 468.

[344] Ibid, 468-469.

[345] *Note:* Some may have wondered why Judge Dundy did not cite Article VI of the United States Constitution in his ruling so that he could then order the government to restore to the Poncas their land taken from them by the "clerical error" of the 1868 Treaty of Fort Laramie. The likely reason is that the matter brought before the court was centered on whether the Application for the Writ of Habeas Corpus should be quashed or confirmed, and whether the arrest and imprisonment of the Ponca prisoners was justified. A narrow interpretation of the issues presented to him, in light of the unprecedented nature of the case, would likely have dissuaded Judge Dundy from ruling on any other matter, even if he personally recognized the injustice done to the Poncas.

[346] *Note:* That Standing Bear was present in the courtroom to hear the ruling is understandable because this was a case of "firsts" (as discussed in Chapter 14). Judge Dundy had already granted Standing Bear and the Ponca prisoners their day in court by accepting their Application for the Writ. He had already allowed Standing Bear to testify as a witness in the trial; and he had granted him the privilege of addressing the court at the end of the trial. Judge Dundy fully understood the historic and unprecedented nature of this case, so allowing Standing Bear and his interpreter Bright Eyes to be present in the courtroom to hear the ruling would be fitting.

[347] O.H. May 15, 1879.

[348] Jackson, Century of Dishonor (1885), Project Gutenberg, Appendix II.

[349] *Note:* The Judges of the United States Circuit Court for the Eighth Circuit for 1879-1880 were identified in *Cases Determined in the United States Circuit Courts for the Eighth Circuit* as: Samuel F. Miller (Supreme Court Justice assigned to the Circuit), John F. Dillon (Circuit Judge for the Circuit), and nine District Court Judges including Elmer S. Dundy (Nebraska), Cassius G. Foster (Kansas), Henry C. Caldwell (Eastern District Arkansas), Isaac C. Parker (Western District Arkansas), Moses Hallett (District of Colorado), Samuel Treat (Eastern District Missouri), James M. Love (Iowa), and Rensselaer R. Nelson (Minnesota).

[350] Jackson, Century of Dishonor (1885), Project Gutenberg, Appendix II.

[351] O.H. May 15, 1879.

[352] Tibbles, *Buckskin*, 203.

[353] Ibid.

[354] Tibbles, *Ponca Chiefs*, 112.

[355] Tibbles, *Buckskin*, 202.

[356] O.H. May 20, 1879.

[357] Poppleton, Caroline, 1915.

[358] Ibid.

[359] O.H. May 17, 1879.

360 Senate Select Committee Report, Testimony of Thomas Tibbles, February 13, 1880, 43. *Note:* General Crook received the Order from Secretary of War McCray to release the Ponca prisoners on May 19, 1879.

361 Howard, 8.

362 Starita, 176.

363 Tibbles, *Buckskin*, 206, 211. *Note:* Tibbles went to Chicago and Boston from June to September 1879 to raise money for the Ponca Relief Committee.

364 Tibbles, *Buckskin*, 212.

365 Tibbles, *Buckskin*, 213-214.

366 Tibbles *Buckskin*, 214.

367 Prucha,184. *Note:* The committee consisted of Fred O. Prince (Mayor of Boston), Levi C. Wade (Speaker of the Massachusetts House), Henry O. Houghton (Publisher), Rev. S. K. Lothrop, B. W. Williams, Henry Mason, Rev. Edward Everett Hale.

368 Tibbles *Ponca Chiefs*, 3.

369 Mathes, *Indian Reform Letters*, 27-28.

370 Ibid, 56.

371 Tibbles, *Buckskin*, 296.

372 Senate Select Committee on the Removal of the Ponca Indians, May 31, 1880, 46th Congress, 2nd Session (Report No. 670), p. xvii-xviii.

373 Omaha Daily Bee, December 4, 1880; *Ponca Tribe of Indians* (plaintiff) *v. Makh-pi-ah-lu-tah, or Red Cloud, in his own behalf and in behalf of the Sioux Tribe of Indians* (defendant).

374 United States Senate, 46th Congress, 3rd Session (1881), Ponca Commission Report, 1.

375 Ibid.

376 Bourke, Diaries, *vol.* 4, 232-233.

377 United States Senate, 46th Congress, 3rd Session (1881), Ponca Commission Report, 39.

[378] United States Senate, 46th Congress, 3rd Session (1881), Ponca Commission Report, 5.

[379] United States Senate, 46th Congress, 3rd Session (1881), Ponca Commission Report, 6.

[380] The Ponca Relief Bill. 1881. 21 Stat. 422.

[381] United States Senate, 47th Congress, 1st Session, Report of the Secretary of the Interior, H.R. Exec. Dir. No.1, 38-40 (1881.)

[382] Wishart, 216; The General Allotment Act of 1887, 24 Stat 388 (1887).

[383] Boughter, 96-120. *Note:* This historian provides a thorough analysis of the ramifications of land allotments in the last two decades of the nineteenth century.

[384] Mathes, *Standing Bear Controversy,* 181.

[385] *Elk v. Wilkins,* 112 U.S. 94 (1884*); State Ex.Rel. Bancroft v. Frear, Secretary of State*, 144 Wis.79, 128 N.W. 1068 (1910); *Appeal of Leah Brunt, Administratix, Estate of Theodore S. Brunt,* United States Board of Tax Appeals, 5 B.T.A. (1926); *James E. O'Neill v. Eldon Morse,* 20 Mich. App. 679, 174 N.W.2nd 575, (1969); *Peter L. Poodry v. Tonawanda Band of Seneca Indians,* 85 F.3rd 874 (Ind. 1996); *Dana Leigh Thompson v. County of Franklin et.al,* 2001 WL 34355597. N.D.-NY. (2001); *Russell Means v. Navajo Nation and United States of America,* 432 F.3rd 924 (CA 2005); *In the Matter of the Adoption of C.D.K., a Minor Child,* 2009 WL 2494618 (D.UT 2009).

[386] Wunder, 60.

[387] Wunder, 44-45, 60.

[388] *Elk v. Wilkins,* 112 U.S. 94 (1884*).*

[389] *Elk v. Wilkins,* 112 U.S. 94 (1884*). Note:* Lambertson discusses the Elk's Case in his article *Indian Citizenship* 20 ALR 183 (1886).

[390] Report of the Board of Indian Commissioners, 1885, 767.

[391] The Indian Freedom Citizenship Suffrage Act (8 U.S.C. Ch.12, Sub. Ch.111, 104, 1b.

[392] Bodayla, 379.

[393] *The Slaughter-House Cases*, 83 U.S. (16 Wall.) 36 (1873), http://www.law.cornell.edu/supremecourt/text/83/36.

[394] *Note:* In Tort Law, the "But For Rule" ("sine qua non") means "without which not" or in other words, it is an indispensable requisite to the outcome.

[395] Tibbles, *Buckskin*, 211-212.

[396] Tibbles, *Buckskin*, 236.

[397] Sheldon, 231; Tibbles, *Buckskin*, 294. *Note:* The date given for the wedding has been listed by other sources as July 23, 1881. However, Thomas Tibbles in *Buckskin* states his wedding occurred on June 29, 1882.

[398] Sheldon, 232.

[399] *Note:* Thomas Tibbles papers can be located at the Smithsonian Institution at. http://collections.si.edu/search/detail/ead_collection:sova-nmai-ac-066

[400]*Note:* United States Office of the Federal Register provided the following information of the Populist Party. It was organized in 1892 and held its first national convention that year in Omaha. William Jennings Bryan was its candidate in 1896 and 1900. Tibbles ran with Thomas E. Watson of Georgia in 1904 and finished fifth out of six candidates with 114,051 votes. Theodore Roosevelt won the 1904 election with over 7,600,000 votes. 1908 was the last election it fielded a candidate.

[401] Omaha Sun, August 7, 1975.

[402] Ibid.

[403] Ibid.

[404] Poppleton. *Reminiscences,* 34.

[405] Green, xi, 97-98.

[406] Wunder, 44.

[407] Bourke, Diaries *vol.* 3, 197-201.

[408] General Crook House Tour Guide.

[409] American Heritage.

[410] *Note:* The term "indifference" was used by the Senate Select Committee on the Removal of the Poncas, 1880 (to read in context, see Chapter 6, Summary in this book). Bright Eyes also used the term "indifference" (to read in context, see Chapter 18, Helen Hunt Jackson in this book).

[411] Wishart, *Unspeakable Sadness*, 243.

[412] Ibid.

[413] *Note:* For additional analysis of the claims process, see David J. Wishart, *An Unspeakable Sadness: The Dispossession of the Nebraska Indians,* 239-245.

[414] *Note:* For more information on the Southern Poncas contact: The Ponca Tribe of Oklahoma, 20 White Eagle Drive, Ponca City, Oklahoma 74601.

[415] *Note:* For more information on the Ponca Tribe contact: The Ponca Tribet 2523 Woodbine Street, P.O. Box 288, Niobrara, Nebraska 68760.

[416] *Note:* For more information contact the Nebraska Commission on Indian Affairs, PO Box 94981, Lincoln, NE, 68509-4981**,** Judi.gaiashkibos@nebraska.gov**,** 402-471-3475.

[417] Olson, 165.

[418] Wolfe, 132.

[419] *Note:* The home addresses of the people involved in "the Omaha Connection," found in *Wolfe's City Directory* for 1878-1879 are: **George Crook**, 596 18th Street. **Rev. H. D. Fisher,** pastor of First Methodist Church, southside Davenport between 17th & 18th Street. **Rev. W. J. Harsha**, pastor of Second Presbyterian Church, corner Dodge & 17th Street. **Rev. E. H. Jameson**, pastor of First Baptist church, southeast corner Davenport & 15th Street. **Andrew J. Poppleton**, attorney 364 Dodge. **Rev. A. F. Sherrill**, pastor of First Congregational Church, northeast corner Chicago & 19th Street. **Rev. T. Henry Tibbles**, asst. editor *Omaha Herald*, northside Mason between 19th & 20th Street**. John L. Webster**, attorney, 380 Chicago Street.

[420] Olson, 13, 25

Endnotes

CPSIA information can be obtained
at www.ICGtesting.com
Printed in the USA
BVHW031119140321
602506BV00013B/658